digital design

digital
design

a critical introduction

dean bruton and
antony radford

BERG

London · New York

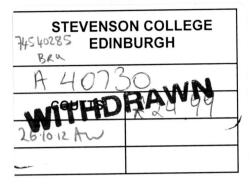

English edition

First published in 2012 by

Berg

Editorial offices:

50 Bedford Square, London WC1B 3DP, UK

175 Fifth Avenue, New York, NY 10010, USA

© Dean Bruton and Antony Radford 2012

Berg is an imprint of Bloomsbury Publishing Plc.

Library of Congress Cataloging-in-Publication Data

Bruton, Dean.

    Digital design : a critical introduction / Dean Bruton and Antony Radford. — 1

        pages cm

ISBN 978-1-84788-828-0 (pbk.) —

ISBN 978-1-84788-829-7 —

ISBN 978-1-84788-917-1

    1. Computer-aided design.   I. Radford, Anthony.

II. Radford, Antony.   III. Title.

NK1520.B78   2012

745.40285—dc23   2012022582

British Library Cataloguing-in-Publication Data

A catalogue record for this book is available from the British Library.

ISBN   978 1 84788 829 7 (Cloth)

        978 1 84788 828 0 (Paper)

e-ISBN 978 1 84788 917 1 (individual)

Typeset by Apex CoVantage, LLC, Madison, WI.

Printed in the UK by the MPG Books Group

www.bergpublishers.com

contents

Rules of the Game

All ordered behaviour, from embryonic development to verbal thinking, is controlled by 'rules of the game', which lend it coherence and stability, but leave it sufficient degrees of freedom for flexible strategies adapted to environmental conditions. (Arthur Koestler, 1964, *The Act of Creation* 96)

illustrations

Plates

Figures

preface

We began with research into the ways that eminent designers and artists framed their work and dealt with unexpected occurrences. That research informed our digital design teaching and our search for ways to link sometimes complex ideas into a coherent theoretical framework. Our text developed through a decade of working with students who took, questioned and ran with these ideas beyond our expectations. The result is a book that we hope will be genuinely useful to students and designers in many fields of digital design.

We thank those students, our colleagues, designers and artists who have made their work available and have been generous in sharing their experience, aims and processes. We owe particular thanks to a few whose collaboration and personal insights have been especially influential. These are Scott Chase, Richard Coyne, John Gero, Neil Hansen, Sabine Hirte, Joan Kirsch, Russell Kirsch, Terry Knight, Ray Lauzzana, Xiong Lu, Mary Lou Maher, Lionel March, John Mitchell, William Mitchell, Kent Neo, Tarkko Oksala, Robert Oxman, Rivka Oxman, Philip Pearlstein, Eric Riewer, Ron Rowe, Peter Schumacher, Denise Scott-Brown, Susan Shannon, Adrian Snodgrass, Tristan d'Estree Sterk, George Stiny, Mark Tapia, Robert Venturi, David Walker and Robert Woodbury. Responsibility for interpreting their words is, of course, ours. We also acknowledge the assistance of numerous institutions including the Universities of Adelaide, South Australia and Sydney, Australia; South China University of Technology, China; Penn State University, USA; Gobelins-School of the Image, France; National Film and Television School, United Kingdom; and FilmAkademie, Germany.

Finally, we thank our partners, Judith Bruton and Alison Radford, for their support and understanding.

chapter 1

---

rules and digital design

This chapter introduces our approach to digital design and designing through rules, pattern and contingency and the idea of designs as part of a language with a vocabulary. We explore how digital representation and computation facilitate an approach to digital design that emphasizes these ideas.

what are the rules in digital design?

This book is a critical introduction to thinking and working in digital design. We explore design with, by or for digital media in any visual field including designed environments (such as architecture and urban design), art, industrial design, film and interactive visual games. We span these many visual fields because a group of core concepts apply to all of them. The purpose of this book is to present this coherent theoretical framework and demonstrate its value to digital designers.

what is digital design?

Digital design is simply design with digital media. Design with digital media is the use of digital processes, graphics and modelling to generate, represent, analyse, evaluate and store design descriptions. Since the 1990s, with the advent of desktop publishing, digital design has largely usurped the use of traditional design media.

design production changes

The design product might be digital or physical. With the Internet, digital radio and television, in

Figure 1.1 Electronic pens and tablets join brushes in the designer's tool kit as digital design changes the traditional design and visual arts studio.

today's world perhaps more designing is done for virtual domains than for the physical world.[1] Where the design product is physical, production is increasingly automated by the direct use of computer aided manufacturing (CAM).

Defining Digital Design

Digital design is the use of computers in the creation of artefacts. The nature of designing has changed since computers began to be used in the process of conceptualization and representation of the design development. Digital drawings and models are immediately editable in ways that are not easily available to traditional media. As William J. Mitchell in *City of Bits* foresaw, 'the uncertainties and dangers of the bitsphere frontier are great, but it is a place of new opportunity and hope' (1995: 173).

Figure 1.2 Rules are found in natural phenomena, as in the way branches and leaves in this plant follow consistent rules that distinguish it from others. Comparable rules can be found in design. Courtesy of Dean Bruton.

a critical introduction

This critical introduction to digital design points out limitations and dangers as well as advantages

> Digital design empowers a designer's use of rules and patterns, but even when a designer is not seeking to impose rules, the media will do so.

of thinking and working with digital media. We are both enabled and limited by any media. We will emphasize the roles of rules and patterns and show that digital design empowers designers in their use of rules and patterns for design production. Furthermore, we will illustrate how rules and patterns pervade all digital designing; even when designers are not seeking to impose rules, the media will subtly do so.[2]

Any critical introduction includes analysis, identification and explanation. We will explain how digital design has compelling advantages, but designers who use it can struggle to cope with what appears to be outside the rules of its software systems. We will see how we need to recognize, welcome and exploit the unexpected, and that thinking in terms of systems and rules is not incompatible with intuition and creativity. The extensive examples from various design disciplines show how the ideas in this book can be genuinely helpful to designers.

In life, the rules that have been imposed on us, and those that we have developed ourselves, are adapted to the special circumstances of each moment. The fact that we are constantly following rules does not mean that we are doomed to follow the same rules in the same way.[3]

We need to see rules as things to be interpreted freely and to see contingency or the chance occurrences of nature as opportunities for creative change and innovative adaption to circumstances.

what is a rule?

A rule is a way things inevitably happen (as in the rules of physics and nature), or the way things are obliged to happen (as in the rules of games and

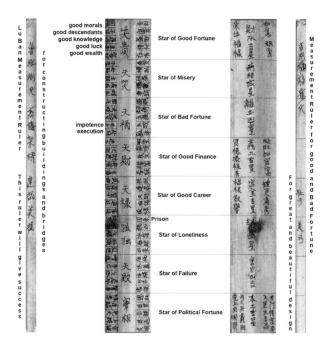

Figure 1.3 Lu Ban Ruler replica (on top), compared to a modern standard ruler. Courtesy of Dean Bruton.

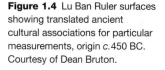

Figure 1.4 Lu Ban Ruler surfaces showing translated ancient cultural associations for particular measurements, origin *c.*450 BC. Courtesy of Dean Bruton.

law), or just the way in which things tend to happen (as in the unwritten rules of a style of art or architecture). We find rules operating everywhere in the world. The uncanny reality of computer simulations reflects the observation and digital representation of rules found in natural phenomena: the ways that creatures move, trees grow,[4] light reflects, water ripples and rock fractures. We shall see that comparable rules mark the products of human design.

rules and patterns and digital design

A pattern is a set of rules. The rules may not be spelled out in words but they are implicit in the pattern. Software routinely includes patterns (alternatively called templates) that provide a starting point for adaptation by a designer.

It is tempting to scoff at these preestablished patterns as undermining the creativity of designers, but designers follow a long tradition of using templates or patterns as starting points for designs. Medieval book illustrators kept pattern books with examples of elaborate page decorations, early equivalents of word processing templates. Carpenters used wood or steel stencils that could be drawn around to define a shape. Tailors used paper patterns to cut cloth for a garment's components. All these patterns could be adapted to suit particular circumstances. Design in the digital age is still guided by patterns.

A word processing template, then, embodies rules for margins, fonts, page format and colours. A carpenter's stencil embodies rules for the shape that will be cut if the stencil outline is followed. But the pattern may not encompass all the rules that define our design. Equally, the pattern may include rules that do not fit in our design.

Figure 1.5 Traditional wooden gulou (meeting hall) in Shanjiang, China, built with the Lu Ban style rule system. Courtesy of Dean Bruton.

Figure 1.6 Stills from *Chronograph* by Tal Rosner and C.E.B. Reas (2011), a dynamic digital mural projected on the wall of the New World Centre, Miami, USA. Courtesy of Casey Reas and Tal Rosner.

In every aspect of life, we tend to start doing whatever it is by following a pattern we have seen or experienced before and then adapting the pattern to suit the situation. It is as if there is a rule that in this situation we use that pattern.

In the early ambitious days of artificial intelligence, rule-based frames and scripts were written to formalize such patterns, so that what we do intuitively could be emulated by computers. But of course, days and situations are not identical. We adapt the pattern to suit the circumstances. While encoding the rules in frames and scripts was relatively easy, recognizing when they apply and how they need to be adapted was and can still be difficult.

In digital design, some of these patterns are drawn directly from precedents in the field of design in which we are engaged. If we are designing something, we look at precedents: if we are designing a Web site, we look for precedents in other Web sites; if we are designing a tap, we look at precedents of other taps.

Architects find patterns in space and construction handbooks, graphic designers in the established styles of fonts, page layouts and image formats. These are precedents, too. They share the characteristic of being whole or partial solutions, pointing to possible ways of doing things (Alexander et al. 1977).

In digital design, we might take a pattern for a Web site from a book, a tree or a river, as well as from another Web site. We might take a pattern for a digital game from a physical sport, a board game or a phenomenon in life that is not usually regarded as a game. Everything we see around us is a potential pattern for our work. If we look at the world with eyes that see patterns, we will build up our own storehouse of unusual patterns that might be relevant for our future designs.

We will see that taking a pattern from one field and using it in another field is one kind of creative action.

This is not mere imitation. Mature designers use multiple patterns that are overlaid and combined. The work of a mature architect, for example, is not obviously based on the patterns provided by past architects, or indeed on the patterns provided in a current handbook of space standards or suggested in the pattern of a leaf or seed. All of these are used, adapted, linked. Over time, the chief source of patterns in designers' work becomes their own previous work.

Designers so thoroughly digest the qualities of many patterns and precedents that the origins are no longer visible. The work of a mature architect or digital designer, for example, is not obviously based on the patterns provided by past designers, or indeed on the patterns provided in a current technical handbook or suggested in the pattern of a leaf or seed. All of these are incorporated, adapted, linked. Mature digital designers do not plagiarize because they use multiple patterns that are overlaid and combined. Over time, the chief source of patterns in our work becomes our previous work.

Figure 1.7 Rules adapt to their context as in the Great Wall of China, seventh century BC, which follows the natural slopes of the mountains. Courtesy of Dean Bruton.

design and the metaphor of language

In developing these themes of rules, patterns and contingency, we use the metaphor of design as a kind of language and apply this to the practice

Origins of Digital Design

Sketchpad (aka Robot Draftsman) was a revolutionary computer program written by Ivan Sutherland in 1963. Sketchpad was the first program ever to use a complete graphical user interface, using an x-y point plotter display and the recently invented light pen. Significantly, graphic user interfaces were derived from the Sketchpad as well as modern object-oriented programming. Digitizers were popularized in the mid 1970s and early 1980s and were used as the input device for many computer aided design (CAD) systems.

Figure 1.8 Designers use graphics tablets in their digital design of a plethora of products. Courtesy of Gray Holland.

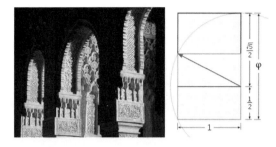

Figure 1.9 Ancient rule systems for proportion (right) were used in architectural design; the arches at the Alhambra (left), Spain, 1338–90. Courtesy of Antony Radford.

of digital design.[5] In an ordinary spoken or written language (known as a natural language), when we think of a pattern of speech or a pattern of writing, we think of the particular vocabularies and compositions that the speaker or writer adopts. The grammar of the language governs the ordered

Figure 1.10 Mogul ceiling pattern at Fatepur Sikri, India, 1570, showing the construction grid rules. Courtesy of Dean Bruton.

way in which a vocabulary of words is modified and combined to convey complex concepts beyond the simplicities of individual words.

In such a language, the vocabulary of words is the set of elements from which the written composition is assembled. By analogy, the pattern of the river in nature encapsulates a vocabulary of water and bank elements that are related according to implicit rules about (amongst other things) levels, transparency, flow and fractal edge. In design, the architectural patterns published in eighteenth-century pattern books encapsulated a vocabulary of stone and timber building elements and rules for their combination.

The templates offered by computer software similarly imbed both vocabulary and rules for how the vocabulary is to be used. For example, the template in a word processor will show a vocabulary of font styles and paragraphs with rules for their combination with margin widths and page lengths. A specialized digital design program for designing seating in a stadium will show a vocabulary of seats with rules for their combination to protect sight lines and access space.

The grammar of a design language can be seen as the way in which a chosen vocabulary of parts is modified and combined in design compositions. We may describe a sculptor as using a vocabulary of wood blocks and stainless steel rods, or a painter as using a vocabulary of layered parallel brush strokes.

We can also think of an architect's vocabulary of brick and timber; a landscape architect's vocabulary of gravel, grass and trees; a musician's vocabulary of orchestral sounds; a scriptwriter's vocabulary of plot, character and action; a Web site designer's vocabulary of fonts, layouts and icons.

We will see that in design it is often not important that a particular vocabulary and rule set are used, but we will also see that the use of a consistent vocabulary and rule set seems to be a generic characteristic of good design.[6] The notion of adopting a restricted or selected vocabulary is common in art, architecture and other design fields, and particularly applies to digital design.

consistency and style

Consistency is a hallmark of the work of successful designers and artists. We can easily recognize the style of major designers because they use consistent rule sets.

In this book we are using terms like grammar *as metaphors*, not claiming that the grammar of design is identical in kind to the grammar of a natural language. When we say that we are looking at designs in a grammatical way, we mean simply that we are looking at the designs in a way that examines the vocabularies and rules that appear to account for a design's form. When we say that a design is highly grammatical, we mean that the vocabulary and rules are very clear. We may also describe such designs as legible, meaning that they can be easily read and understood.

If we claim that there is a grammar for a design, we are claiming that there are not only consistent rules and vocabulary, but that the rules and vocabulary work together to make coherent wholes that are expressions in the language defined by the grammar. Designing in the same grammar will result in designs that belong to the same language. There is an overlap between this use of the terms grammar and language and the more common use of the word style.

Grammar highlights awareness of form, repetitive patterns, constituent parts, and compositional rules, while language highlights families of

The Digital Age

The digital age is a time when people use computer technologies as a fundamental part of the way they understand and operate in the world.

Internet technology began to be used in the 1960s; the Internet and Transmission Control Protocols were initiated in 1973, and the World Wide Web was developed from 1989. Prensky (2001) distinguishes between younger 'digital natives' who have grown up with the media and know and accept its characteristics on their own terms, and older 'digital immigrants' who have migrated to using digital media and continually compare its characteristics with those of traditional media.

designs that share common formal features, and the idea of designs suggesting meanings. They are well-used metaphors: there are books about the grammar or language of art, sculpture, ornament, architecture, landscape architecture, advertising, wood and vision.

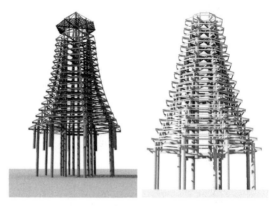

Figure 1.11 Exploring form using generative algorithms: variations in designs for a gulou created in Grasshopper software with a grammatical approach that offers alternative digital design structural options, 2010. Courtesy of Xiong Lu.

Figure 1.12 Contingent
juxtaposition of shapes generated
with Joshua Davis's online
programs and digitally collated
together. Applying digital designs
to commercial products facilitates
innovative manufacturing.
Courtesy of Dean Bruton.

meaning and digital design language(s)

Can art and design have meanings in the way that we expect of a spoken or written language? A design field in which there has been much discussion about meaning is architecture. Peter Smith states unequivocally that 'architecture conveys messages; it is a medium of expression that, like language, relies upon an agreed code' (1987: 9).

Roger Scruton objects that 'if it were true that architecture were a language (or, perhaps, a series of languages), then we should know how to understand every building' (1979: 158). Scruton's statement assumes that we know the language and can understand what is expressed in the language. Often, neither is true with natural languages, so we can hardly expect this to occur when confronted with art and design languages. In architecture, we may not be able to understand the meanings of buildings that originate outside our culture and time in the way that those familiar with the buildings' languages understand them. Even then, though, we may find many meanings in the building because our own experience and ways of looking might find elements of the building richly evocative. The meanings for us do not necessarily coincide with any meanings intended by the building designers.

So too in digital design the meaning of a design may not coincide with the original intention of the designer.[7] Digital architecture carries this same tradition of associated meanings into the virtual world. Indeed, designers of virtual environments often base their designs on physical worlds in order to associate the established meanings of familiar architectural and urban spaces.

Little of the relationship between the language of digital design and its meaning is clearly articulated. Indeed, Gunther Kress and Theo van Leeuwen lament the 'staggering inability of most of us to talk and think in any way seriously about what is communicated by means of visual images and design' (1996: 16). John Lansdown and Rae Earnshaw assert this point:

> Art works such as musical compositions, poems, paintings, dances and so on do not carry messages in the same clear cut way as everyday prose. Decoding them is usually not easy—nor is it meant to be. Ambiguity and multiple meanings are inherent in such things. (1989: 67)

Figure 1.13 The languages of many design fields have been the subjects of books. Courtesy of Antony Radford.

computers and parametric design

We have noted already that all computer software is rule-based. Here, we want to show how digital designs can be derived if we are precise in our rules and vocabulary, in the way that computer algorithms are precise. We will consider three rules that say a rectangle in a design can be replaced by a pair of rectangles or a coloured rectangle.

Parametric design is about describing designs and their parts in terms of relationships. The relationships are themselves rules. Consider a line:

we could define it as joining two variable points which might move, or as joining two fixed points in space. In the former case, if one or more of the points move, the line adjusts its length and angle to continue to link the two points. In the latter case, it does not. In our small set of rules, then, all the lines are parametric. If we re-scale or change the proportions of the whole image, all the relationships continue to apply.

We could take this further. We could have a rule that if the format of a rectangle is horizontal (landscape), it will always be filled with a blue colour; if it is vertical (portrait), it is always filled with a red colour. This rule defines a relationship

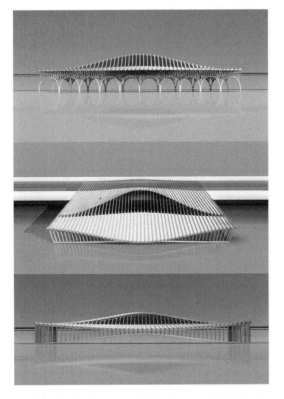

Figure 1.14 Three variations (above) towards a final design (below) for a railway station in Guangzhou, China, 2010. Courtesy of Leng Tianxiang.

between the geometry and an attribute of a surface defined by that geometry. There are many other relational rules we could introduce. For example, we could have a rule that if the aspect ratio of a rectangle is more than 4:1, it will always be divided into two rectangles. These kinds of relationships are analogous to the kinds of operations and rules that can be set up in a spreadsheet, where the whole sheet is automatically updated when any change is made to the contents of a spreadsheet cell because of the relationships that have been defined.

A spreadsheet needs repairing if we break a defined relationship by erasing cells or putting the wrong kind of data in a cell; the whole sheet goes awry because a relationship is broken.

Similarly, in parametric design we do not just add to and remove from the design; rather, we can also relate parts of the design description to other parts and (as a consequence) may also need to repair the design description if we break these relationships (Burry 2006; Woodbury 2010).

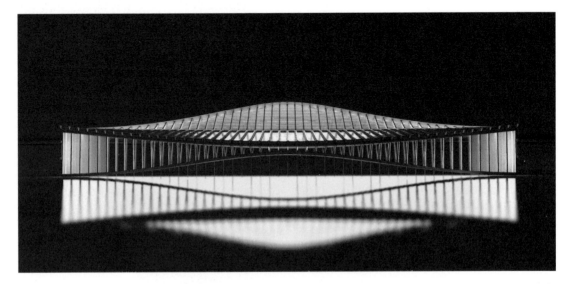

Figure 1.15 Final design for a railway station in Guangzhou, China, 2010. Courtesy of Leng Tianxiang.

Parametric design is one of the ways in which digital design is different from design with old media: we can think about relationships when we draw lines with a pencil on paper, but we cannot get the whole drawing to reconfigure itself if we move one of our lines. Parametric relationships are built into much design software (as well as spreadsheets), and we may also be offered the means to define our own parametric relationships.

implementing rules in digital design

A computer program that implements our small set of parametric rules is Mondrimat, by Stephen Linhart, a Web designer (Linhart 1998). This is one of a number of Web sites that allow visitors to create their own (somewhat) Mondrian-like art works.

One of the most easily recognized (and most emulated) languages in fine art is that of the artist Piet Mondrian's (1872–1944) paintings after 1920 (Deicher 2010). If we consider a corpus of these works, we might say that they all follow an obvious pattern. They have a vocabulary of rectangular coloured shapes and black lines that are combined using rules of rectilinear composition, proportions, relationships and colour.

An individual painting in Mondrimat is derived in a sequence of stages by the addition and modification of the vocabulary elements according to the rules, and all the designs derived in this way are members of the language of these paintings.

The narrow constraints imposed in Mondrimat might be seen as an extreme projection of Mondrian's own career as an artist, during which he imposed increasing constraints on his choices as

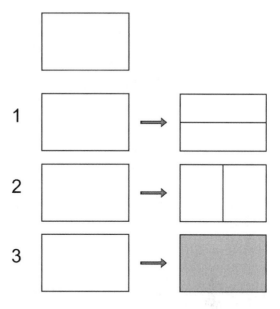

Figure 1.16 Representations of replacement rules use arrows to show that if the shape on the left-hand side can be found in the design, then it can be replaced by the shape on the right-hand side.

Figure 1.17 Mondrimat, 1998. Courtesy of Stephen Linhart (http://www.stephen.com/mondrimat).

Mondrimat Rules

The simple controls for the program are these:

1. Click on the right 1/3 of a colour block to split it across.
2. Click on the lower 1/3 of a block to split it up and down.
3. Click anywhere else in a block to change its colour.
4. Drag the frame dividers to resize blocks.

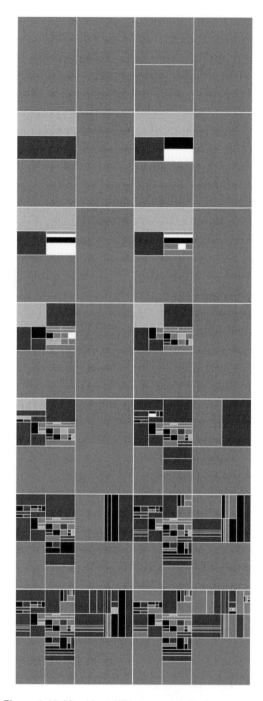

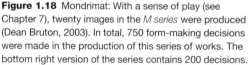

Figure 1.18 Mondrimat: With a sense of play (see Chapter 7), twenty images in the *M series* were produced (Dean Bruton, 2003). In total, 750 form-making decisions were made in the production of this series of works. The bottom right version of the series contains 200 decisions.

a way of exploring directions that had emerged from his previous work (Harrison 1978: 146).

Looking at examples that can be generated on the program's Web site,[8] some results appear quite Mondrian-like, while others appear far from Mondrian—there are other rules at play in the artist's own work. Nevertheless, some of the innumerable images that this restrictive rule set generates are visually appealing.

We could follow the same rules in making designs by hand without Mondrimat, but the number of designs in the language that we explored would probably be far fewer.

One of the benefits of using digital media is the ability to explore quickly. The number and richness of design possibilities that a formal grammar of any sophistication encompasses is beyond manual exploration. So far there are few computer programs that directly implement grammar concepts, and most of those that do exist take just one predefined grammar, rather than offer their users a means to define their own grammars. The experience of those who have gone down this path helps our understanding of the nature of rules, vocabularies, grammar and language.

CAD-CAM

Computer aided manufacturing (CAM) began with numerically controlled (NC) machine tools. In 1948, the first automated machine tool used punched paper cards to control the tool. Later, researchers at the Massachusetts Institute of Technology built the first true NC machine tool in 1952. The first computer aided design (CAD) systems were an outgrowth of the early CAM work. Systems which combined the design of mechanical parts with their manufacture by NC mill and lathe machines were designated CAD-CAM.

rules, understanding and designing

Scruton notes that for lovers of architecture, 'it is a pleasure founded on understanding, pleasure which has an object, and not just a cause' (1979: 112). Overlaid on the visual experience of looking at surfaces and volumes and the kinetic experience of moving through spaces is an experience of interpreting and understanding the architecture. Knowledge usually adds to pleasure; the kinaesthetic pleasure of dancing is heightened for the enthusiast by knowledge of (the rules of) technique, understanding of (the rules of) choreography, and the memory of (the patterns of) other dances.

Scruton contrasts architecture with wine, arguing that for both expert and novice, the enjoyment of wine is essentially a 'gustatory pleasure' that 'does not demand an intellectual act' (1979: 112). We disagree; there is indeed a sensory pleasure in drinking good wine, but there is also an intellectual pleasure in recognizing the winemaker's skill, the region of origin, the influence of the balance of grape varieties and the effect of aging. We enjoy reading the bottle's label—about the rules of cultivation of the grape and its transformation into wine—as well as drinking the contents. The recognition of rules is important to our enjoyment of architecture and art because, like a fine wine or a piece of music, we want to understand how it might have been created and how it relates to other work. So the pleasure of experiencing architecture is a direct sensory pleasure and is also considered an intellectual pleasure, the 'object of pleasurable attention' (1979: 73). This pleasure applies equally to digital design, art, music and other form-making activities and is linked to the ability to explain to ourselves what we are experiencing.

Figure 1.19 Parametric glasses of virtual wine constructed with variations on a three-part vocabulary of bowl, stem and base. Courtesy of Tim Forbes.

Paul Valéry connects explanation and making in this way:

> To explain is never anything more than to describe a way of making: it is merely to remake in thought. The why and the how, which are only ways of expressing the implications of this idea, inject themselves into every statement, demanding satisfaction at all costs. (1956: 117, qtd in Karatani 1995: 24)

We will understand the design works of others much better if we 'remake in thought'. Indeed, the act of criticism has been seen as an imitation of the act of creation but an act seeking insights that were missed by the creator. Such insights can occur in re-understanding our own design work when we return to it after a break.[9]

digital design and the characteristics of digital media

Having introduced the particular way we want to describe design and designing in this book (through rules and contingency and the idea of designs as part of a language with a vocabulary), it is time to look at how the special characteristics of digital representation and computation facilitate an approach to digital design that emphasizes these ideas. The following list (developed from Manovich 2001: 27–48) highlights six features by which digital media differ from conventional media.

1. Ubiquitous representation

All information (images, text and sounds) is represented as code, essentially a pattern of binary choices (a bit) which we can think of as 1 or 0, yes or no, present or absent or on or off. We refer to digital media and digital design because we generally think of this code as digital. This ubiquitous form of representation allows for the easy distribution, combination and transformation of information.

In digital design, this code itself is never inspected; it is always a new and fresh expression as image or sound, or less commonly tactility, that is presented and used. This expression is the result of rule-based transformations, and the same code can be represented in different ways according to the rule-based transformations that are carried out.

Moreover, the plurality of possible relations between code and its presentation works both ways, so that the same image or sound can be represented in different ways. For example, an image of a three-dimensional object may be generated from data that digitally represents a collection of pixels, lines, surfaces or solids. How we change and develop the image depends on our choice of representation. This means that when choosing and using software in digital design, we need to think in terms of what information about our design and its contexts needs to be represented.

2. Transformation

As well as allowing a code to be expressed as an image or sound, rule-based mathematical functions can change the data into new data. Transforming the code, of course, transforms the represented image or sound.

Transformation also makes possible parametric and procedural design descriptions that can

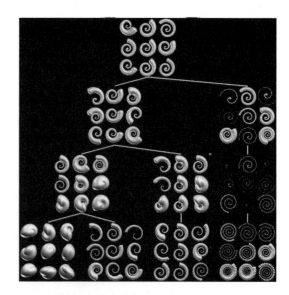

Figure 1.20 Stages in the development of a biomimetic form, 2010. Courtesy of William Latham.

fit many situations or be used to explore options. This means that when choosing and using software in digital design, we need to think in terms of what kinds of transformations might be useful in developing our designs.

3. Multiple versions

From these basic characteristics of ubiquitous representation and transformations, it follows that information rarely exists in a unique form. Instead, it exists in many forms and versions including databases, prints, hypermedia and update versions. As a corollary, earlier versions of the information can be retrieved and transformed in different ways.

In digital design, we need to think in terms of multiple versions of our work in possibly different forms. One of these forms might be the information needed to control a 2D or 3D printer or production machine such as a lathe, router or cutter. This links the design information directly with the production information. Other forms of the information might relate to different aspects of the design.

In building information modelling (BIM), a single model of a building is the origin for multiple representations suited to briefing, design, evaluation, construction and operation-in-use stages in a supply and management continuum. The same principles and benefits of integrated information modelling and management apply to all design fields. In the digital design studio collaborators might be in different parts of the world and share the same design model, in either the same or different versions. If we are collaborating, the transfer and sharing of information is far easier with digital media, and if we all use the same basic model we know our work will be consistent.

Figure 1.21 Instances of virtual bottles generated by parametric modelling using Genoform. Courtesy of Genometri Ltd.

4. Modularity

The collective term *digital media* encompasses many modules that do different things. In preparing a document, for example, we will typically use different modules for image manipulation, text processing and page layout. Each module facilitates the application of rules within its area of application. We need to think in terms of developing a design in stages, where in each stage we use the most appropriate software module. We can also think, if we wish, of designing with traditional media as a module or stage in a process that also includes designing with digital media. We do not have to be purists and forsake the pleasures of sketching with pencil and paper.

In mixing digital and manual media, we can start with hand sketching and then transfer that information to a digital representation. This is common. In art and graphic design we could also end with a module of hand drawing over a print from a digital image. If, though, we try to move from digital to non-digital and back to digital design representations we have to be very careful that all the relevant information in the original digital model is reinstated.

5. Interface

If these modules are to link together, the interfaces between them must work. This means that data produced as output from one module must be available in a form that can be input for the next module. In the world of digital design, much attention is given to interoperability and the setting of data representation standards so that different systems can work together. Digital design also requires many of these modules to interface with humans. While we rarely think about the interface between us as designers and the paper on which

we make a pencil sketch of a design, the means by which we can turn our imagined forms into representations in a computer is an important issue. For example, if we want information to flow from design to production stages, sufficient information must be defined to make this possible. If we simply scan our hand-drawn sketch, we will have to add a lot more information, including defining the geometry more precisely.

The means by which those computer representations are made apparent to us is similarly important. If we want to see the results of some computer-generated form design, those must be visible to us in 2D or 3D. Interfaces are themselves designed, and they set up patterns and rules that are followed. Gradually, digital design has followed trends that make human–computer–human interfaces more direct and less inhibiting.

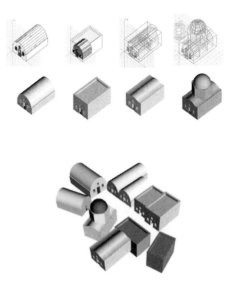

Figure 1.22 Constructing a vocabulary of building forms: based on traditional patterns from Santorini, Greece. Courtesy of Antony Radford.

Figure 1.23 Instances of virtual spoons generated by
parametric modelling in Genoform. Courtesy of Genometri Ltd.

6. Automation

Processes that a human carries out individually
with traditional media can be automated in digital media. At times during digital design, human
intentionality may, in part, be removed from the
creative process by initiating a rule-based procedure that can be extensive in scope. The combination of automation and the ability to safely
return to earlier versions encourages a try-it-and-
see design strategy. Indeed, one strategy in digital
design is simply to use algorithms (a sequence
of rules expressed as a process) to automatically
generate lots of designs or partial designs and
then pick those to develop, either by ourselves
or via equally automatic evaluation algorithms. We
need to think in terms of a partnership between
our human processes and automated processes
for design generation and design checking. We
also need to think about responsibility and author-
ship and the appropriateness of auto-generative
processes to our design situation.

four assertions about digital design

In digital design, then, we are implementing
innumerable rule-based actions within the media
that store, transmit and sometimes automatically transform the information that describes our
designs. If we can join these actions with human
creativity, we have a means to empower designers, link them so that teamwork is more effective,
and give them more direct control over the form
and quality of the final product.

Figure 1.24 Zapxcov, a design derivation generated by an evolutionary parametric modelling program. Courtesy of William Latham.

We end this chapter with four linked assertions about digital design.

1. Understanding the roles of vocabulary, rules and patterns can make the use of digital media more effective

Many artists and designers react warily to the term *rule* as suggesting something too fixed, too rational (Walker 1996). It seems to contradict romantic stereotypes of artists as rule-free radicals. Nevertheless, 'anyone learning how to paint, write music, poetry or the skills of architecture' will 'inevitably find that the learning of recipes, principles, rules of thumb and more exact rules for achieving varieties of effects and results' will be just as prevalent as in any 'less exalted' trade or profession (Harrison 1978: 60).

The interpretation of each moment of the design continuum is enhanced by recognition and understanding of the rules and vocabulary that are in use. The designer is empowered by this recognition. In digital design, we have to link our own rules with those of the computer software and attend to their compatibility.

The recognition that contingency means that there may be turning or change points in the progress of design leads to the second assertion.

2. Revealing the contingency of vocabulary and rules can expose moments of inspiration and redirection in a reflective design activity

The points where a pattern of design development changes are significant in any design endeavour. These are points where the design is being re-framed, where different possibilities are seen. Digital media provide arenas for the construction of 2D and 3D compositions that may be examined and recorded through the conception and construction phases, and through the ease of transforming and recording images, highlighting both continuity and apparent sudden changes in the development of designs.

The third assertion relates to globalization, collaboration in the virtual studio and the digital workflow through design and production.

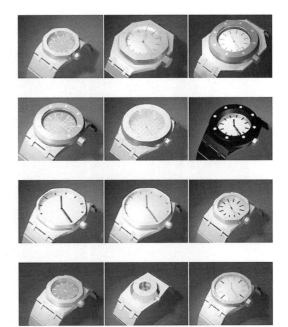

Figure 1.25 Instances of virtual watches generated by parametric modelling, generated using Genoform. Courtesy of Genometri Ltd.

3. Being explicit about vocabulary and rules assists in learning about design and the collaborative efforts of dispersed groups

It is easier to learn if we know the design language we are trying to speak, and easier to share effort if everyone speaks the same design language. An analogy is what happened in the artists' studios of the Renaissance, where assistants were able to paint in the language of the famous masters by understanding and mastering the grammar of their work. More recently, the most effective of

Figure 1.26 Rail simulation, a serious game that trains staff in the procedures to follow in the event of an incident within the London Underground. Courtesy of Sydac Pty Ltd.

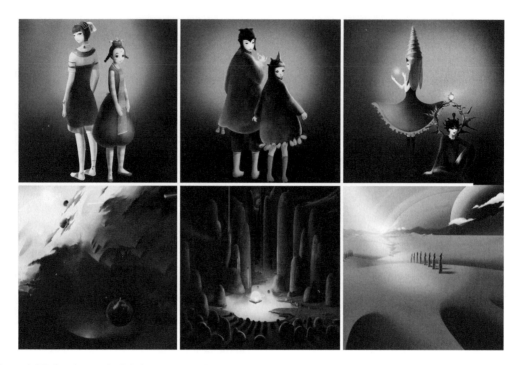

Figure 1.27 Consistency in digital character design (top row) and set design for film (bottom row). Courtesy of Angela Kim.

famous international architectural offices achieve productivity by having ways of doing things that everyone understands.

With globalization and the sharing of work between offices and people that never physically meet each other, the common grammar needs to shift from something acquired unconsciously through close working contact to something articulated and disseminated. But this is not the only reason to be explicit.

Figure 1.28 Auto-generation of a tree using ContextFree, 2010. Courtesy of Xiong Lu.

4. Being explicit about vocabulary and rules is required in the automated exploration of alternatives and the linking of design with production

Exploiting the potential of digital processes and representations in parametric and algorithmic design and exploring options (sometimes called 'optioneering' [Holzer and Downing 2010]) similarly requires clarity in the definition of rules, patterns, vocabularies and grammars.

Finally and most obviously, to couple design and manufacture in a continuous digital workflow also requires precision. We cannot tell the numerically controlled machine to make the cladding panels 'about this size' of 'something' with fixing holes 'somewhere over there'. At least, not yet.[10]

Summary: Rules of the Game

Designers typically respond to design opportunities by using patterns and following rules that seem to fit the situation. The most common source of these patterns and rules is their own previous work. But these patterns and rules are not immutable things that reduce designing to the routine following of predetermined prescriptions. Instead, they are starting points rather than answers, and always need interpretation in the specific context of their use. In digital design, the designer's rules are accompanied by the media's rules, and the two sets must be compatible.

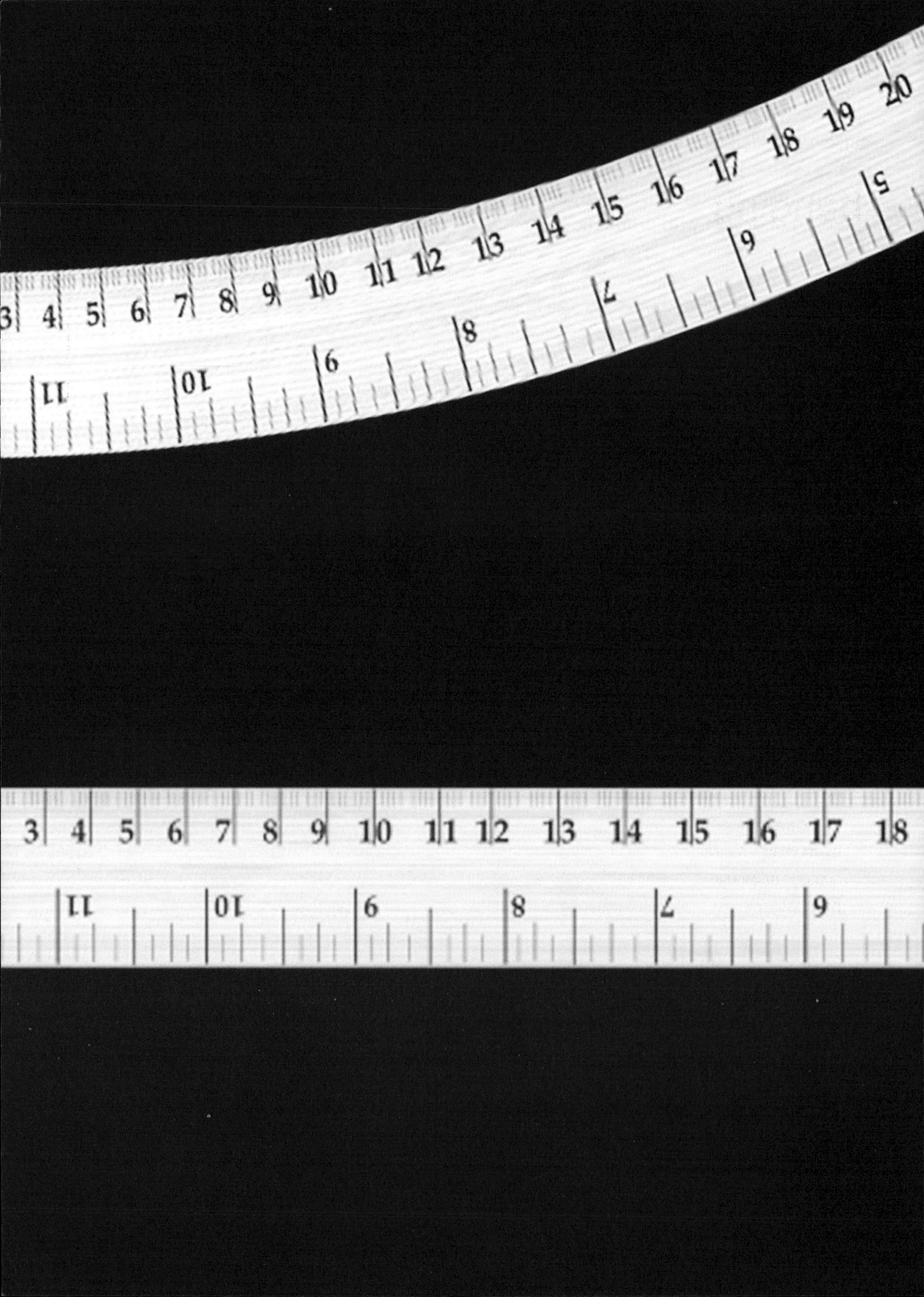

chapter 2

bending rules

In this chapter we frame rules as contingent and argue that a contingent sense of design grammars and patterns is enabling rather than restrictive. We recognize implicit assumptions in digital design about inherent computational vocabularies and rules, and suggest designers match these assumptions in the way they use media in practice.

how does contingency intervene in the operation of design rules?

If life and the way the world operates could be explained and predicted by rules alone, the world would be a far less interesting place. Rules can describe regularities and consistent relationships but cannot predict outcomes.

> Even in a chess game, you cannot use the rules to predict 'history'—i.e., the course of any given game. Indeed, you cannot even reliably predict the next move in a chess game. Why? Because the 'system' involves more than the rules of the game. It also includes the players and their unfolding, moment-by-moment decisions among a very large number of available options at each choice point. (Corning 2002: 14)

Consistency is disrupted and the rules of the general and the past must be adapted to the particular and present. Life is contingent, and we need to be prepared to deal with contingency.

The smart digital designer is one who welcomes contingency, welcomes the challenge of

Figure 2.1 Bending virtual rules—reframing the design situation in a particular way. Courtesy of Dean Bruton.

the unexpected and the spur it provides to be inventive.

reflection in digital designing

Any sustained creative endeavour is a reflective practice. We all recognize the voice we hear in the back of our head when making important design decisions.

Reflection is a contingent inner discussion with oneself whereby we call forth experiences, beliefs and perceptions in relation to our activities. In digital design, processes of anticipation, action and evaluation of the results of that action are intertwined in a hermeneutic[1] process of increasing understanding.

We need some sense of what we are trying to do, but this may be the vaguest of ideas.

> In order to understand one must 'fore understand', have a stance, an anticipation and a contextualization. This is what is known as the 'hermeneutic circle': one can only know what one is prepared to know, in the terms that one is prepared to know. (Lye 1996: n10)

In order to create, one must similarly fore create—have an anticipation of the created work or idea, however intangible and evasive. There must be purpose, an idea of what is sought.

Figure 2.2 Generative design following rules based on the drip paintings of Jackson Pollock using jacksonpollock.org, 2010. Courtesy of Dean Bruton.

The designer frames the design situation in a particular way and hence predicts (however hazily) the design outcome in a particular way.

This anticipation of the created work does not close down the possibilities because of our constantly self-reflective nature. We see new possibilities. While we begin with particular expectations, these are revised during the process of making as rival ways of seeing emerge. We are influenced by what we make and respond by making a new version.

Any 'process worthy of the name "creative" will involve an in-eliminable interaction with "intermediary" products which themselves help to create the psychological states of the creator' (Briskman 1981: 93). Yet we generally act as we think, immediately, as the direct outcome of thought (Harrison 1978: 44), much as we speak as we think rather than rehearsing sentences in our minds.[2] For example, as soon as the painter-as-doer makes a mark on a canvas, the painter-as-thinker sees what is there and decides the next mark. Whether we paint with a brush or make an image with digital media, we do so in a continuous process, only occasionally pausing to reflect.

These processes in the work of professional architects, medical doctors, lawyers and town planners are described by Donald Schön in his influential book *The Reflective Practitioner.* He writes that the process may be unconscious or subject to reflection: 'At the same time that the inquirer tries to shape the situation to his frame, he must hold himself open to the situation's backtalk' (1982: 164).

As a sequence of decisions or choices are made and assimilated, the work becomes a record of these choices with their own logic and consistency (Harrison 1978). Indeed, this consistency comes to drive further choices. It seems that the way that the design has developed dictates the way that it should continue to develop. In grammatical terms, the increasingly defined grammar of the design determines how the continuing design is written.

This is intrinsic to a sense of grammar in creative action—the vocabulary and rules adopted in early decisions come to suggest and constrain the vocabulary and rules for later decisions.

Sometimes the stages are apparent in the finished product. In some artwork—such as Jackson Pollock's celebrated drip paintings (Emmerling 2003), where dribbles of paint lie under or over each other depending on the order of their placement—the product itself declares the order of decisions in its creation. Digital design media often automatically record this sequence of actions, so that it can be unwound again by Undo commands.

Design, then, is a reflective process of thinking and doing in which a product, system or service develops. In this development process, the materiality and form of the partially developed product talks back to the designer. The designer's next action is not entirely predictable, but rather contingent on this talk back and other aspects of the situation. The expected pattern of development is sometimes disrupted, and the response is contingent to this disruption.

It is the contingency—contingent on the interplay of idea and materials, on new understandings of what has gone before, on innumerable possible events that trigger a small or major reframing of the situation—that opens up the possibilities, that invites renewal and discovery. Contingency pervades everything we do and who we are. Philosopher Richard Rorty goes so far as to describe the self as 'a tissue of contingencies' (1989: 32). So, inevitably, contingency 'infects every design task'

(Johnson 1994: 257), regardless of the chosen media.

adapting patterns

We have noted that the most common source of patterns in a mature designer's work is his or her own previous work. This is to be expected: the most common source of patterns in any human activity is previous experience. Schön explains that professionals 'see' a situation as similar to one that they have encountered before. This does not mean, though, that they can merely reapply the same pattern. *The situation is never exactly the same.*

Along with similarity there is difference. Patterns, taken from any source, need to be modified to suit the contingency of the situation. Put another way, the patterns need to be bent to fit. Bending the pattern means bending the vocabulary and rules. Schön explains this adaptive action:

> When a practitioner makes sense of a situation he perceives to be unique, he sees it as something already present in his repertoire. To see this site as that one is not to subsume the first under a familiar category or rule. It is, rather to see the unfamiliar, unique situation as both similar to and different from the familiar one, without at first being able to say similar or different with respect to what. The familiar situation functions as a precedent, or a metaphor, or . . . an exemplar for the unfamiliar one. (1982: 137–8)

This notion of 'both similar to and different from the familiar one' has a parallel in taking patterns from outside our personal experience as well.

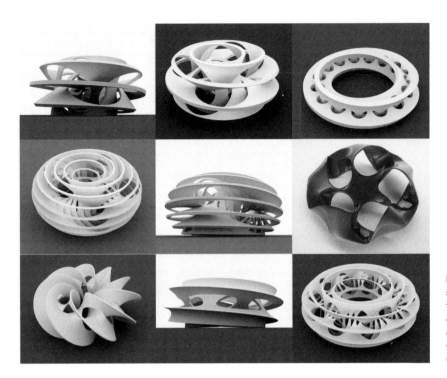

Figure 2.3 Variations of self-intersecting mobius forms with parameters of numbers of twists, circuits and holes using Grasshopper, 2010. Courtesy of Xiong Lu.

When we use a pattern from nature as a pattern for our design, we see the possibility of the patterns being in some ways similar while not denying differences. If we start to see the thing we are designing as something else, then it opens up our awareness of the patterns associated with that something else. *Alternative digital design possibilities emerge.*

contingent design vocabularies

The choice of vocabulary is much more important than merely choosing between equally appropriate ways of expressing ideas, because what can be expressed is intimately related to that choice.

A design vocabulary is contingent in the sense of depending on what is available, what preconceptions exist and how whole design and art fields perceive the nature of appropriate vocabularies. Debate in design is rarely about the pros and cons of different ways of using a given vocabulary, and more often about the emerging use of unexpected and new vocabularies.[3] The work of eminent designers and artists (at different times) such as Zaha Hadid, Jackson Pollock, Frank Gehry, Philippe Starck and Damien Hirst—citing only some obvious examples—is recognizable as much by their radically different vocabularies as by their compositional rules.

changing the design game

It is generally harder to change vocabulary in the course of design than to change rules. We tend to think in terms of a particular vocabulary and not stray far from it, so our vocabulary becomes an unacknowledged constraint on what we do.

Yet some vocabularies allow some kinds of expressions better than others. It is fascinating to listen to a conversation between two people who are both bilingual, and how they switch from one language to another depending on which is better suited to express what they want to say.

Despite the difficulty, during the course of a single design, designers may amend their design vocabulary. In our journal record for our own design work in Chapter 8, we refer to an initial vocabulary that is modified as a part of our reflective practice.

Over time, designers may switch vocabularies more radically, as in the painter Mondrian's switch to a more geometrically formal vocabulary of his later paintings, the architect Edwin Lutyens's switch at the turn of the nineteenth and twentieth centuries from a vocabulary drawn from the elements of picturesque English rural architecture to one of what he called 'the great game, the high game' of classicism, or the Web designer Joshua Davis's adaptation of his vocabulary to suit commercially productive online digital design formats.[4] In all these cases, the vocabulary is modified to better match the design aims.

contingent rules

In design, practical rules are analogous to the rules that govern the conduct of societies or games, giving rise to inexhaustible possibilities of interpretation and action (Snodgrass 1991: 6). Given the pervading nature of contingency, all such rules are subject to interpretation in different ways in different situations.[5] This means that a rule must be re-understood each time it is applied, in a way that takes into account the particular situation.

In everyday life grammar is taken for granted: parents do not teach their children the rules of language; they simply talk to their children and correct mistakes when each child begins to speak. The parents may not know the rules of language in any codified sense, but they can practice them.

Further, in language and games—and design— the rules are never exhausted. The range of possibilities contained within the rules allows games, languages and design their richness, spontaneity and fascination. So design rules are rarely applied twice in exactly the same way because any number of contingent factors contributes to endless variations in the design process.

software rules

When we initiate a rule in computer software— scaling a dimension, changing a colour, generating a digital design—we contingently choose to

Figure 2.4 A tree finds a crevice in which to grow as a tissue of contingency. Courtesy of Antony Radford.

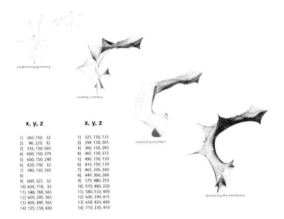

x, y, z	x, y, z
1] 260, 150, 32	1] 325, 150, 135
2] 96, 220, 32	2] 294, 150, 205
3] 335, 150, 565	3] 360, 150, 293
4] 600, 150, 370	4] 465, 150, 335
5] 600, 150, 240	5] 490, 150, 130
6] 420, 150, 32	6] 410, 150, 130
7] 540, 150, 565	7] 465, 295, 340
8] -	8] 440, 366, 268
9] 600, 325, 32	9] 570, 480, 250
10] 600, 710, 32	10] 570, 480, 250
11] 548, 760, 565	11] 580, 530, 400
12] 600, 295, 565	12] 600, 390, 415
13] 600, 495, 565	13] 658, 430, 480
14] 725, 150, 430	14] 710, 330, 410

Figure 2.5 Stages in the generation of complex membrane geometry in Rhino software. Courtesy of Bartolomeo Maiorana.

Figure 2.6 Interior of Chinese long houses parametrically modelled and generated in Grasshopper. Courtesy of Xiong Lu.

Rules and Contingency in Digital Design

For humans, the word 'rule' suggests a fixedness and clarity that it does not have (Harrison 1978: 79), at least in design. Practical design rules are not objective, nor are they applicable in the same way in each design case.

apply such apparently *a priori* rules and make subtly different interpretations about how to apply them in every case. Consider computer programs that do apparently design autonomously, whether by following inbuilt procedures or by executing a series of designer-defined rules. Is there a hermeneutic process going on within the computer system? No, unless one attributes human-like qualities to computers (we are reluctant to do so).

Is there a hermeneutic process going on when a human uses such computer systems in design? Of course there is; *all design is hermeneutical.* The computer program is not the whole of the design situation, which always involves humans. A computer program is used, modified, and perhaps steered in a hermeneutic process. So the essentially hermeneutic nature of design does not prevent a designer from exploring (within a hermeneutic process) the deterministic operation of a sequence of rules (Woodbury 1993).[6]

Instead, deterministic, algorithm-based operations in software programs are seized upon by creative users to produce results that no one would dream of making without such programs.

Available media have always influenced artists' products and aspirations, but with digital media, the transformations tend to be more complex, more encompassing and less predictable than is common with traditional design media. Moreover, 'numerical models [in computer software] have the unfortunate disadvantage of containing no information about when their contents are appropriate' (McCullough 1998: 106). Since such models are always a part of some larger system of interacting parts, there should always be provision (and responsibility) for another part of the system—the human part—to establish appropriateness.

Fortunately with design in digital media, there is often the luxury of deciding appropriateness after rather than before the event—try it and accept or reject the outcome by simply returning to an earlier stage.[7]

contingent meanings

The way we interpret designs is also contingent. In natural language, the meaning of even a single word depends on time, place and usage. The philosopher Ludwig Wittgenstein's well-known comment that 'the meaning of a word is its use in the language' highlights that *we know the use or rule of language practically rather than theoretically.* A written text is 'not only a construction of time and place and outlook of the author, but also those of other authors, and also (on each occasion) of a reader' (McCullough 1998: 90). As designers, we can try to make our work meaningful to those who see or hear it, but it will be interpreted differently by each person.

In a famous lecture called 'The Creative Act' delivered in 1957, the artist Marcel Duchamp said this:

All in all, the creative act is not performed by the artist alone; the spectator brings the work in contact with the external world by deciphering and interpreting its inner qualifications and thus adds his contribution to the creative act. This becomes even more obvious when posterity gives its final verdict and rehabilitates forgotten artists. (77–8)

We quote this because it draws attention to two ideas: the importance of the relationship between the work and the spectator, and the way that relationship can change over time. This is relevant for all design products. But there is an aspect to this statement that is not immediately apparent: the artist and the spectator might be the same person. The artist's performance is deciphered and interpreted by the artist when she or he revisits the work. Our own partially completed designs may be interpreted differently by ourselves as designers.

As we make images (by hand or digitally), we interpret those images. Sometimes we see them differently: a shape that emerges from the overlap

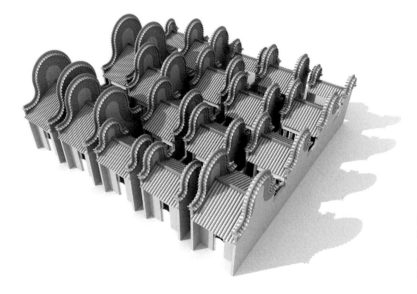

Figure 2.7 Chinese long houses parametrically modelled and generated in Grasshopper. Courtesy of Xiong Lu.

of two other shapes might seem important, might suggest a new way of developing the design. Others might prompt this re-interpretation. Many a design tutor in an architecture school has turned a student's model on its side and suggested that what had been the façade of the building could work as the plan.

Being open to finding new meanings in and interpretations of what we see and make is a characteristic of creative thinking. What emerges in the representations of the developing design is also supplemented by what we see and experience elsewhere. If we are thinking intensely about our digital design, we begin to find patterns and ideas in the wider world that seem relevant. We can appropriate these, manipulating them to fit into our design.

emergence: the downside

This phenomenon in which new shapes and forms emerge during the process of designing is very important, and we need to be open and receptive to it. If we take elements and combine them, we may produce something that has properties quite different from those of the original elements; an often cited analogy is the combination of oxygen and hydrogen as water. What emerges is often surprising. But we need to be able to think in terms of the new element and not be forced to continue to think in terms of the original elements. If we insist on seeing water as oxygen and hydrogen, with all the properties of oxygen and hydrogen, we might never see it as a drink.

There is an issue here for digital design. We have seen that amongst the characteristics of working digitally are those of multiple versions and automation, and that the way information

is described determines what can be done with that information. There is a huge advantage in the downstream linking of design and production to be specific about the elements and their properties. Similarly, the use of design information for visual and performance simulation relies on being specific.

A visualization needs to know about surface reflectance and translucence, while a thermal analysis of a building needs to know about materials and their thermal properties (interfaces are made to make the definition of geometry and properties as easy as possible, but it is still a lengthy task). Indeed, design software may be highly specific about the vocabulary elements that are recognized and how they must be described. Trying to make a visualization of water with software that only allows the description of the reflectance and translucence properties of oxygen and hydrogen would be challenging.

Imagine, then, the disruption to all this investment in the digital model of the design under development if we suddenly think that no, what was always intended to be two separate rooms in the plan of a building will now be appropriated as the shape of a single courtyard. Instead of just thinking yes, that's a great idea and moving on with the next sketch, we would probably have to delete the rooms and their enclosing walls and repair the design model by making new elements for the courtyard and its surrounding walls.

Will this discourage us from making a change that would improve the design? It may. With analogue, paper-based media, a student's final presentation drawings were typically done at the last minute, and there was little difference in effort between tracing an earlier version and drawing a new version. The surprise of radically different proposals was common: students had come to

Figure 2.8 Dissolving into another: a tree responds to its context as it grows; *Buddha Tree*, Ayuthaya, Thailand, 1974. Courtesy of Judith Bruton.

Value of Awareness in Digital Design

Good digital designers are aware of the formal structures, ordering systems and even rules that permeate the process of designing. They are aware that designs do not spring unheralded in final form but derive in some way through a series of studies and developments. They are aware that the work of some artists and designers exhibits a clearer, more articulate form than that of other designers. They are also aware that these things are contingent, depending on circumstances. They do not see any of this as inhibiting their creativity.

emergence: the upside

There is an upside, too. With parametric design and automation, we can discover design outcomes that we might never imagine with analogue media. In what is sometimes called *emergent design*, we can take found data that is drawn from another source (examples are a page of text or statistics, or the energy consumption of a city) and interpret it as geometry. More commonly, algorithms are used to generate designs in an open-ended process to produce numerous design forms that are often surprising.

We can choose from what is generated and develop it further. We can also couple some kind of evaluation algorithm to the generative algorithm so that the system itself selects what is best from the candidates that emerge (As and Schodek 2008: 173). Evolutionary algorithms mimic the processes of natural selection in the biological world in a rapid cycle of generation, evaluation and selection.

In a typical process, many candidate solutions are automatically generated based on rules and genes (starting parameters). The results are ranked by an evaluation algorithm (or human

---

thoroughly understand the design issues and had seen better ways to respond to them. With digital media, the final presentation images are refinements to and modifications of earlier versions. Students may well still see a much better way to respond to the design issues, but creating a new digital model is daunting. Similar issues arise in practice.

The freedom to see the developing digital design in a new way is related to the ambiguity of the representation: the more ambiguous, the more likely we are to make lateral and unexpected interpretations. Ambiguity, though, is anathema to mobilizing all the rule-based power of computation.

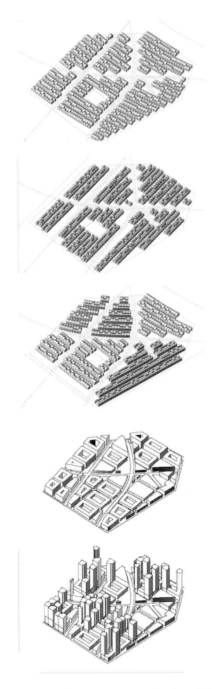

Figure 2.9 Exploring various patterns for urban design subject to the contingency of road layouts, generated using Grasshopper software, 2010. The top three are a row house typology with various orientations, the fourth is a perimeter block typology, and the fifth is a mix of perimeter blocks and point blocks. Courtesy of Xiong Lu.

intervention, which is always a possibility when the kinds of quantitative measures that can be applied automatically are inappropriate and human judgement is needed). The so-called genes of solutions with high rankings are then recombined with others by swapping some of their parts, or mutated by making a small change to a single element. These are then used in another cycle, generating and ranking new solutions (Bolliger, Grohmann and Tessmann 2010: 36).

The idea is that successive generations are based on the gene pool of the best solutions of the previous iteration. The cycles continue until there is little difference between the generated solutions, or until the process is arbitrarily stopped. Evolutionary algorithms do not make any assumption about the underlying form of the design outcomes, but they are inevitably constrained by the kinds of designs that can result from the rules and genes in the system—they assume a design language.

The terms *genotype* and *phenotype* are sometimes used. A genotype is a design's heritage through the cycles, even if not expressed. A phenotype is its properties, such as its form and behaviour, which can potentially be evaluated. As in biology, it is the properties of the phenotype that determine a candidate design's chances of survival and reproduction in the next cycle, while the inheritance of these physical properties occurs only as a secondary consequence of the inheritance of genes in the genotype.

These algorithms are particularly useful when there are many variables and the generation of potential solutions by systematic changes to those variables in a parametric process is unwieldy. The design outcome, though, is the responsibility of the human designer. When these processes are used merely to generate visual form, the process itself may be interesting, and knowledge of the

Figure 2.10 Stages in the progressive subtraction of material to make a more efficient structure using an evolutionary optimization algorithm. Two different sequences are shown: a group of six columns (left, with a rapid prototype model in wax alongside) and a pair of columns (below). Courtesy of the Innovative Structures Group with the Spatial Information Architecture Laboratory, RMIT University: Peter Felicetti, Jiwu Tang and Mike Xie with Jane Burry and Mark Burry.

process may add to our enjoyment of the design. There is almost nothing intrinsically better about basing visual form on the outcomes of generative algorithms than on any other means of generating form: the shards of a broken plate, perhaps, or the splatter of ink on paper. We need to judge whether it is appropriate.

contingent instances

The patterns developed during design may themselves have to be adapted for particular situations; an example we will see in Chapter 6 is a cladding panel which instead of being fixed in size and curvature needs to be different for each panel on a building façade. If we can define the panel as relationships,

then we can handle this issue during design and during the later production of the panels.

A parametric design description is often an algorithm rather than a drawing or model; a single algorithm can produce many designs. Writing an algorithm, though, involves scripting or programming according to the rules of the script or program language. 'Designers, especially well-prepared to deal with ambiguous, ill-defined

Stage 1

Stage 3

Stage 5

Stage 7

Figure 2.11 A rule-based generated simulation of the mediaeval urban form of the city of Granada, Spain, by generated interpretation. Courtesy of Mansoor Ma.

Figure 2.12 A sequence of transformations of a tree image, starting from top left. Courtesy of Claire Kearton.

problems, suddenly [have] to come up with unambiguous, well-defined, formal descriptions, syntactically correct to the last semicolon' (Scheurer 2010: 89). A common strategy for designers who find this hard to do is to work with others who enjoy the challenge. The payoff is evident and lasting: if we can make a parametric or algorithmic design description that can adapt to different positions in a project, we may also be able to re-use the same design element in another project.[8]

evolution and change

The personal grammar of a designer, or the grammar of a wider style, develops in design and art practice in two ways:

1. When a designer follows a similar theme or process but changes an aspect of the work such as the media, location, construction or other identifiable contributing factors
2. When a designer introduces a new rule or vocabulary element in the course of the production of a work

We have noted that during their careers, many designers and artists do contingently change the

grammar with which they work. In the history of design and art, ideas of paradigm shifts, the avant-garde and the so-called shock of the new signal change and revolution. Rudolph Arnheim comments on the characterization of styles and their boundaries:

One of the most stubborn and awkward ways in which the practical mind interferes with the seeking of the truth consists precisely in replacing types with container concepts based on the staking out of territory. In art history, for example, one can gain genuine understanding by defining styles, such as Expressionism or Cubism, as pure types of attitude and manifestation and by showing how in a given artist such ingredients combine in a particular blend. In that way, one begins to understand the history of art as a fluctuating interplay of underlying types of approach, by which a particular pattern comes to the fore at some time or place or in some person, only to dissolve into another. (1969: 177)

This dissolving into another can be seen in all design fields. In the history of Western architecture, for example, the transition from Norman to Gothic and from Gothic to Renaissance is marked by buildings that blend elements of the later style into buildings that continue many of the themes of the earlier style. Moreover, there is a sense that this transition is because the old style is not working any more, is not able to express the aspirations of the time. 'The birth of a new concept,' writes Edward Sapir, 'is invariably foreshadowed by a more or less strained or extended use of old linguistic material' (1921: 17, qtd in Arnheim 1969: 245).

If changes in design styles are considered in terms of vocabulary and rule addition, deletion and changes, turning points become easily identifiable. Turning points are both starting and ending points. They concurrently encourage reflection on past actions and future directions.

We can illustrate this with a story about how analysing a designer's work—something we address in Chapters 5 and 6—does not necessarily predict what that designer will do next. In the early 1980s, Australian architect Glenn Murcutt (later the 2002 Pritzker Prize laureate American Institute of Architects Gold Medallist) was best known for a series of pavilion houses in rural New South Wales, Australia.

The vocabulary of the houses is clearly based on a long, pitched-roofed pavilion, roofed and often walled in uncoloured corrugated steel. This distinctive vocabulary was accompanied by some consistent rules about building relationships with the ground, roof form, structural grid and internal spatial division. Neil Hanson formalized the vocabulary and rules as a grammar for their generation based on an analysis of Murcutt's designs and the then available writing by and on Murcutt and his work.

Hanson tested the grammar by designing a house by following the rules of this grammar. The derivation of form in any architecture is contingent on its site and the spatial requirements of the client, and in this case he was able to use a site for which Murcutt had been commissioned to design a house. Hanson also obtained some briefing information from the client.

Although not intended that way, a derivation in these circumstances could be seen as an attempt to predict what Murcutt would do in the given circumstances. The design derived was for a single

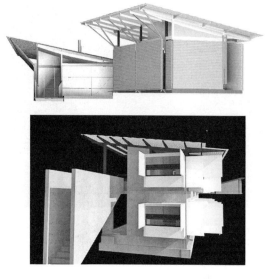

Figure 2.13 Adaptation of Glenn Murcutt's architectural language for a house to a larger building: Simpson-Lee House, 1989–94, and Arthur and Yvonne Boyd Education Centre (with Wendy Lewin and Reg Lark), 1995–9. Images of digital models constructed by Poppy McNee and Verdy Kwee, University of Adelaide.

pavilion with north-facing external deck. Murcutt's reaction to the rules of the grammar and the design of the house resulting from the derivation is relevant here.

Murcutt said this of the grammar: 'But this won't show me the future, the next design, it is only interested in the past.' He commented that a 'wrong rule' in the list was that the grammar 'did not project the use of a garden shed', referring to a low-cost tubular steel pipe system which had not been used in the corpus of designs that were examined. He said that if he used such a rule set, his designs would never improve, never develop; he could only produce variations of his past designs. He said he was always refining his ideas, building on what he had done in the past, but without his own natural input, nothing original could arise. Murcutt said, 'I carry all those ideas

Figure 2.14 Sphinx group of moths showing the combination of consistency and variation in the rich evolutionary variety of nature. Courtesy of Stephen Rannels.

Figure 2.15 Apparently organic form generated by an evolutionary algorithm and selected in response to personal aesthetic references, *Mutator*, 2008. Courtesy of William Latham.

big rock shelves) meant he had to use different solutions.

In his later work, Murcutt has continued to steadily refine and enrich his distinctive personal grammar. There is both consistency in the whole corpus of his work and clear changes over time. His larger projects, such as the Arthur and Yvonne Boyd Centre south of Sydney (with Wendy Lewin and Greg Lark), adapt the language of his houses to the scale and presence of public buildings.

around with me in my head' (qtd in Hanson and Radford 1986: 72).

On contingency, Murcutt commented that if the general rules could not be applied, he found others, citing a house which broke all the rules because other factors (the lie of the land and

Figure 2.16 Adapting design to contingency: the design for the House of Culture in Helsinki (1952–8) by architect Alvar Aalto that required the late addition of a film projection box. The wall of the building bulges out to make room for the box. The lower photograph shows how the ceiling inside the hall has been modified to leave room for a duct. Both have become amongst the most photographed parts of the building. Courtesy of Antony Radford.

keeping a record: digital journals

Keeping a journal supports reflective making. Regardless of the medium that is used, both the process of making a journal and the process of accessing it later prompt self-reflection and reinterpretation.

There is a long tradition of designers and artists keeping personal journals or notebooks in which they record ideas and note what they see that might be relevant for their future work.

For the digital designer, a digital journal typically includes the documentation of ideas and sketches, drawings, sound bites, diagrams and multimedia. A digital journal can be much more complete than a physical journal because digital designers are able to accurately archive the development of each idea by saving files to a hard drive or portable storage device. The impact of

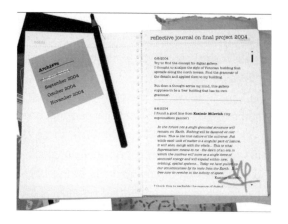

Figure 2.17 Electronic journal keeping for reflective practice in digital designing. Courtesy of Deviana Sutandi.

contingent interventions, serendipitous events and accidents is more easily assessed in a digital journal.

This means contingency can play a more distinct and distinguishable role, and we can celebrate the development of creativity and innovation.

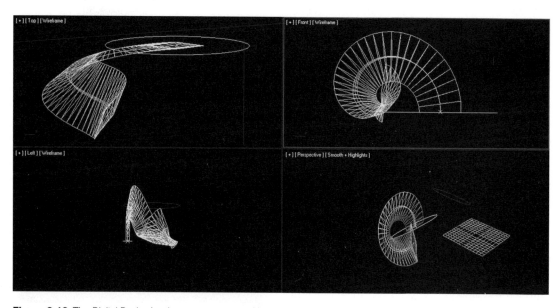

Figure 2.18 The *Digital Design* book cover was created in a 3D application offering four possibilities. The turning point in the design process was the selection of one solution for development. Courtesy of Dean Bruton.

Online digital journals are also effective for communication to the public or, if need be, to a client via password access. The private journal then becomes a published blog.

In Chapter 8 we will describe the generation of some of our own work in digital design, based on our own digital archives. Originally, these records were kept using a personal perspective and voice. During the many drafts of this book, this record has lost some of its immediacy, but we will try to retain traces of our different personalities and priorities in the way we describe what we do.

rules, contingency and media

Rules may suggest that there is something fixed, a certainty. In this chapter, we have framed rules as contingent and argued that a contingent sense of grammars is enabling rather than restrictive. The fact that the rules of law and science also suggest a determinacy that is not borne out in their application does not limit their usefulness. Yet we have recognized that digital media themselves make assumptions about rules and vocabulary, and effectively ask designers to match these assumptions in the way they use the media.

As Bryan Lawson writes, 'Having to work with a computer tool that does not represent knowledge the way you do may cause considerable interference in your thinking' (2004: 71).

Computer tools are frequently restrictive, but our response if we are going to harness the benefits of digital media in design must be to adapt both the media and our ways of thinking. In the terms of philosopher Warrick Fox (2006), we need to seek a kind of responsive cohesion in our design processes as well as in our designs.

Figure 2.19 Bending rules: design rules for constructing a traditional wooden (fir) gulou are reinvented for a modern Chinese stadium used for bull fighting and concerts, Shanjiang, Liuzhou, Library of Guangxi Zhuang Autonomous Region, China, 2010, architect Wei Dingjin. Courtesy of Dean Bruton.

For our design media, we should choose a combination of what we feel comfortable with, and what offers most in the efficiency and effectiveness of the whole design, production and management continuum. Over time, though,

Figure 2.20 Freeform digital architectural design akin to a natural landscape: Opera House, Guangzhou, China, 2003–10, architect Zaha Hadid. Courtesy of Dean Bruton.

digital media will get better at seamlessly transferring ambiguous design information into fuller design descriptions for processing. At the same time, new designers will inevitably tend to think in ways that are symbiotic and not in conflict with the characteristics of their preferred design media, and that is increasingly digital.

In the next chapter we will explore how rules and contingency interact in some different fields of digital design.

Summary: Bending the Rules of the Game
The consistency of rules is disturbed by the unpredictability of contingency. A pattern rarely repeats in the same way as it has done before, just as natural disasters disrupt life and personal events influence digital design decisions. Awareness of this—the occurrence and modification of potential patterns within design languages—can assist the smart digital designer.

chapter 3

—

making digital artefacts

In this chapter we will look at some of the subfields of digital design. This allows us to discuss the interrelation of the vocabularies and rules imbedded in digital media with the vocabularies and rules espoused by the designer in the context of these particular subfields.

how do rules and contingency interplay in different fields of design?

In the first two chapters we argued the design benefits of a focus on rules and contingency and examined the characteristics of digital design media in these terms. So far, what is being designed has been of lesser importance; these pervasive concepts will apply whatever is being designed. Now we focus on specific kinds of artefacts. We shall begin with what might be called digital objects: outcomes of digital design, art and architecture, and how they are depicted in static images and flybys, with single and multiple views. We then turn to digital stories: digital animations, game art and films where time plays a role in an unfolding narrative.

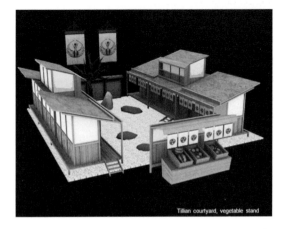

Figure 3.2 Virtual space design: built environments are a key part of a computer game design language. Courtesy of James Pearse.

Figure 3.1 *Moon Hare*, still from a short animation combining hand-drawn and digital animation design. Courtesy of Betty Qian.

Figure 3.3 *Beast*, a chaise longue by Neri Oxman in collaboration with Craig Carter, Museum of Science, Boston, 2010. As a chaise longue, the surface contingently responds to the human body. When stood upright, the same form takes on meaning as a long-necked beast.

Next we look at digital places: Web sites, virtual worlds and the environments for digital games where instead of being a passive observer of predefined (re)presentations, the audience is positioned as an active participant in its own story. This is a new phenomenon with digital media; conventional media using analogue technology (film, video, vinyl records and audiotape) cannot support interactivity (Miller 2004).

We should explain these distinctions. The digital object is conceptually static, like a view of a painting or sculpture or building. The digital story is conceptually moving, changing over time like a film. The digital place is conceptually an environment to be visited, explored and even manipulated, like a night club or a sports field where neither route nor views are prescribed. The digital game adds aims, structure and rules of play to a digital place.

But once having drawn these distinctions, we should immediately blur the edges. The way a digital object is presented—imagine a well-directed sequence of static and moving views—can tell a story. The way a digital object is made—how a final version is derived from precedents and earlier stages in its development—is also a story. The way we play a digital game—imagine a session where we pit our wits and skills against dragons and devils—creates a story. As soon as we introduce notions of time and change, there are stories to be told.

Digital objects

When designing digital objects, we need to be aware of the vocabulary of elements and the rules by which those elements are joined and modified. We have drawn attention to this in the preceding chapters. The vocabulary and rules may transcend a transition between the real world and the digital world.

Figure 3.4 Digital timepiece as virtual object. Courtesy of Jacob White.

Figure 3.5 Visual effects scene construction in a folio Web site presentation, combining real and virtual elements. Courtesy of Archie Dowell.

Figure 3.6 Landscape architecture: proposed sculpture series based on subtractive operations on a cone, Adelaide, 2010. Courtesy of Tanya Court and Xiong Lu.

Consider taking a photograph and manipulating it with pixel-based image software such as Photoshop, Gimp or similar applications. There are vocabularies and rules in what we choose to picture and how we decide to compose the image. The vocabulary may involve such simple decisions as what is foreground, what is background, which are the shapes in two dimensions and what is the play of light. The important point is to ask, what is the vocabulary in this image? The rules may involve camera angles and positions. Consider a photograph of a human face, perhaps a self-image. The conventional rule would be to compose the photograph with the face in the centre, the typical head-and-shoulders composition of a passport photograph. More striking images might be sought by adopting a different rule: low angle, very wide angle. Again, the important point is to ask, what are the rules in this image? Now we open the image file. We can think in terms of the vocabulary of a face: eyes, nose, mouth and ears. But the vocabulary the software knows about is different. It knows about a vocabulary of colours and layers, and about rules of transformations,

substitutions, merging and filtering. To exploit the software's capabilities, we need to think in terms of this vocabulary and these rules, too.

And the really important message is that to get the best overall outcome, we need to be aware of the vocabulary and rules of the software when we compose the original image, because we make possible transformations and manipulations by the way we make that image. The sequence of composing the photograph and manipulating the image becomes a story in itself, and it can be fascinating to look back over that sequence. In Bowl Series in Chapter 8, there is an extensive presentation of such a sequence where the art work is this story and is not just the final image.

Where is the contingency in this process? Contingency intrudes at every stage: the lighting is not quite as anticipated, the transformations are not quite as expected, the printing changes the colours a little. Some, probably most, of these unexpected happenings will be regarded as nuisances and lead to repetition of the stage. A few will present unexpected and occasionally extraordinary outcomes that will be welcomed. Either way, we

Figure 3.7 The interface for the Web site of *MUJI*, a Japan-based product retailer that uses a restricted number of consistent design elements, 2011. Courtesy of MUJI.

have to do the best we can with whatever contingency throws at our work. And it is surprising how often our response to that contingency leads to a better outcome than would have otherwise occurred.

The conventional photograph or picture is a single, static image. The digital image invites multiple views: details, enlargements, transformations to convert the singular into a series. In these transformations, the vocabulary and rules may be themselves transformed. But not necessarily: an enlarged detail of a digital image on a computer screen retains the surface qualities of the original with only the scale changed.

We do not try to design buildings with Photoshop, Gimp or similar desktop publishing applications because a pixel image system cannot adequately represent the kinds of vocabulary elements and rules that are needed for buildings. Object-based drawing and modelling systems are better. Specifically, building modelling systems are even better because the vocabulary elements recognized in the software are explicitly the same as the vocabulary elements of a building, and the rules are explicitly appropriate for buildings.[1] The

Figure 3.8 Hand sketches, 3D digital model and rapid prototype physical model of a hand-held fruit and vegetable slicer. Courtesy of Michael Ng on behalf of Daka International Ltd, Hong Kong.

On Desktop Publishing

Jill Yelland writes,

> In the 1970s a technological revolution burst upon the typographic scene, in the form of the computer. This affected everyone, from the designers to type manufacturers. The earliest computer-based typesetters were a hybrid of photocomposition machines and, by the 1980s, pure digital output. None of these early machines handled graphics well and all had their own font formats. By the late 1980s the development of desk top publishing (DTP) changed the face of typography and the printing industry worldwide. (1996: 9)

difficulties are different. When a building designer seeks to use vocabularies and rules that are unconventional in building, and thus not anticipated by the software designers, it becomes harder to get this synergy between the software design medium and the real object being designed. This drove Frank Gehry's architectural office to use a modelling system originally intended for the kinds of vocabularies and rules found in aerospace and automotive design.

The key idea is the linking of different representations and versions of an object so that the form becomes just one of many types of information about the object. On a small scale, we shall want to link our design model to a 2D printer, or to a 3D printer for rapid prototyping production of physical models from 3D digital files. These allow us to, say, hold a proposed mobile phone in our hand instead of just seeing it, for even 3D visual presentations lack the touch-and-feel of a physical prototype.

Figure 3.9 Rigging control systems for a dragon follow rules and patterns for facilitating successful animation.
Courtesy of Daniel Bigaj.

Figure 3.10 *Vegetarian nightmares*, virtual 2D visualization of prototypes for 3D modelling. Courtesy of Dean Bruton.

graphic design

Rules and patterns have pervaded graphic design since medieval monks laboriously copied decorated manuscripts. We have noted already how desktop publishing software continues this tradition by offering templates for document layouts. The advent of digital design has enlarged the range of design outcomes and design practice. For example, Stefan Sagmeister's Web site menu includes work in Film, Identities, Books, Installations, CD Covers, Posters, Editorial, Promotional, and Furniture, invading areas hitherto understood as foreign territory.[2] In parallel, software and templates for graphic design have spread from 2D to 3D space.

As in other fields, digital graphic design has both encouraged standardization and enabled difference. The ideas of vocabulary, rules and meanings are well established in graphic design. For the formalists promoting standardization, we cite the work of Massimo Vignelli, and for the anti-formalists promoting difference, we cite Milton Glaser. The former emphasizes universal rules and the latter emphasizes contingency, the importance of responding to specific situations.

Vignelli described his design style as 'spare, essential, intellectually elegant, strong, timeless (at least I hope!)'.[3] 'Syntactic consistency,' he writes, 'is of paramount importance in graphic design as it is in all human endeavours' (Vignelli n.d.). When working in the Vignelli studio, Michael

Figure 3.11 Cumulus typeface design: first ideas (top) and completed alphabet (bottom). Courtesy of Augusta Lindquist.

Industry Applications

What happens when we use digital media to design something that is to be produced outside of digital flatland—a building, a car, a sculpture or teapot? Nothing fundamental changes, but there is a lot more to handle. We still need a vocabulary and rules, and we need to consider their relationship to what the computer software knows about.

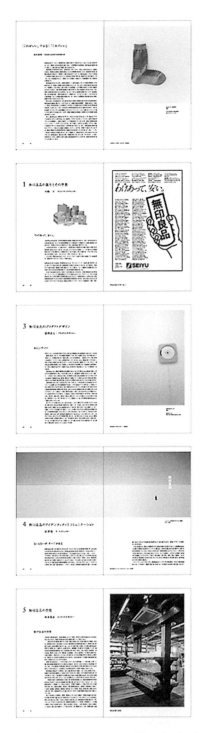

Figure 3.12 Format, typography and layout rules for a *MUJI* catalogue design, 2011. Courtesy of MUJI.

Bierut (2011) listed the 'things he was not allowed to do' as he began his first job:

- Use any typeface other than Helvetica, Century, Times, Futura, Garamond No. 3 or Bodoni.
- Use more than two typefaces on any project.
- Use more than three sizes of typefaces on any project.
- Begin any layout without a modular grid in place, including a letterhead or a business card.
- Make visual references to any examples of historic graphic design predating Josef Muller-Brockmann or Armin Hoffman.
- Incorporate any graphic devices that could not be defended on the basis of pure function.

Bierut (2011) recalls,

Massimo once told me that one of the great aspects of modernist graphic design was that it was replicable. You could teach its principles to anyone, even a non-designer, and if they followed the rules they'd be able to come up with a solid, if not brilliant, solution. To me, this was both idealistic—design for all—and vaguely depressing, a prescription for a visual world without valleys but without peaks as well. Sometimes impulsiveness and self-indulgence were no more than that, but every once in a while they were something you might call genius. I worried about genius.

In the introduction to his book *The Vignelli Canon*, Vignelli counters: 'It is not the intention of this little book to stifle creativity or to reduce it to a bunch of rules. It is not the formula that prevents good design from happening but lack of knowledge of the complexity of the Design profession. It's up to the brain to use the proper formula to achieve the desired result' (Vignelli n.d.: 6).

By contrast, Glaser points to appropriateness for specific situations as the principal goal. Glaser (2011) argued that

> it would be hard for somebody looking at the range of things that I do to see a persistent pattern in them, except in the realm of drawing and illustration . . . where the choice of colors and forms are more obviously personal. I have the idea that there isn't any truth in style. It's very temporal, bound to the moment that we live in and the way we see things. If it's useful to you, fine, if not you move on to something else.

John Maeda (2011) deliberately resists consistency. 'I try to keep changing. I don't like to be labeled as a certain style, so I continue to destroy everything I did, maybe every few months. My wife is the reason why, she always says, doesn't that look the same? She's the pressure that keeps me changing.' Rune Pettersson similarly emphasizes contingency by titling his 2010 book on information design *It Depends*. Sagmeister, however, found avoiding design rules and patterns became impossible:

> For a long time we prided ourselves not to have a style, which to uphold became impossible. This is because if you really switch your stylistic approach from project to project it is impossible to come up with a new one on a weekly or monthly basis, without ripping-off either historical styles or a particular designers' style.

Figure 3.13 Rules for consistency (top), and some contingencies to consider in font design (bottom). Courtesy of Augusta Lindquist.

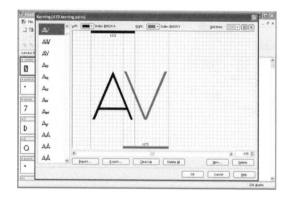

Figure 3.14 Kern pair. The Cumulus design process involves many decisions about spacing of form. Courtesy of Augusta Lindquist.

Figure 3.15 Cumulus family. Courtesy of Augusta Lindquist.

Regardless of any stylistic concerns, a digital designer must consider the variations on a theme or formal concept. Often a previous idea dominates the design at first. The use of analysis to

FINAL CONCEPT: PixelForce Digital

Business Cards   **Letterhead**

Figure 3.16 Graphic design process showing the variations leading to a final business card design for PixelForce. Courtesy of Hinney Lo and Tim Jupe.

break down the idea into vocabulary and rules, as in the design of a business card or letterhead, enables the design to coincidentally develop in a rational and intuitive way.[4]

GIS, UIS and BIM

The data needed for graphic design are few compared with those needed for descriptions of cities and buildings. Geographic information systems (GIS) and urban information systems (UIS) are primarily databases about land and urban places, so we can typically find information about (for example) land use and ownership, area, utility services and values. Amongst this information are 2D and 3D representations, so we can see maps, plans and 3D visualizations of places as well as numeric and text data. The combined model can be used to derive statistics and to find (for example) what is in sunlight at a particular time, what can be seen

Figure 3.17 Decorative print for a Reebok shoe that followed Maeda's third law of simplicity and was designed using his original mathematical algorithms and computer codes, 2008. Courtesy of John Maeda.

from a particular point and from where that point can be seen.

For design, all this provides a means to explore 'what if . . .?' questions about the future: what if a proposed new building is constructed, what if land values dramatically change, what if population grows or drops? The same model is then used as the basis for understanding and recording the present and for exploring the future. Incorporating time as well as form (versions of a 3D model for the past, present and possible future) is often referred to as 4D modelling.

Building information modelling (BIM) is transforming the processes by which buildings are designed and built. It has long been argued that one of the problems of buildings is that there are rarely prototypes: the final building is also the first attempt. Moreover, inconsistencies and clashes in the data are common: the engineers' drawings show one thing, the architects' drawings another and a ventilation duct tries to go through a column.

BIM offers an integrated digital prototype through which problems can be identified and

Transformation and Digital Objects

The notion of a digital object, as an unchanging, discrete object, is almost an oxymoron. The digital is always open to transformation, to viewing in different ways, to exploration, in a way that the physical is not. We can present multiple views of the object on a computer screen. We can use animations to track changing viewpoints. If we think in terms of vocabulary and rules, then that suggests how to drive the animation: a vocabulary of image types and rules about image placement and transitions. We shift from displaying an image of a designed object to telling a story about a designed object.

solved. As in urban and land information systems, the description of form and geometry is a part of but not the entire model. Typically, there is also information about building components, materials and surfaces. For example, along with its geometry, the information about a heating unit might include data about its clearance requirements, capacity, supplier, cost, operation and maintenance procedures.

Figure 3.18 BIM, building information model (Revit), of Mount Barker Waldorf School Living Arts Centre designed by Troppo Architects. Courtesy of Victor Cai and Troppo Architects.

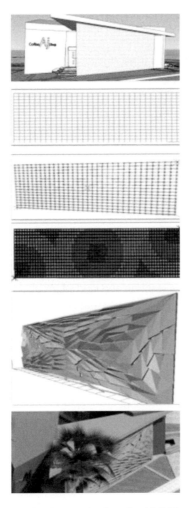

Figure 3.19 Wall design using Paracloud GEM for a restaurant proposal in Jeddah, Saudi Arabia, 2011. Courtesy of Yasser Almutiri.

activities. Examples are modelling of foundation and excavation scenarios, analysis of construction sequence alternatives, and creation of digital mockups of alternative structural and curtain wall system designs. The model continues into the construction phase, being updated to reflect responses to contingencies that arise and being used to look ahead to the next construction operations.

In virtual architecture there are no such issues. We can choose our vocabulary with an eye on the capabilities of the software. The designers of virtual architecture exploit this freedom, so that their work is dominated by vocabularies of free-form curving surfaces transformed and joined by rules prescribing tenuous, delicate links, vocabularies and rules that are anathema to the realities of structural strength and constructional feasibility in the architecture of the real world.

digital stories

Storytelling is a fundamental cultural cornerstone, the ancient method of passing on information and wisdom. Oral storytellers do not memorize a set text, but rather learn a series of script-like incidents that form a story line (a plot) with a distinct beginning, middle and end. The teller mentally visualizes the characters and settings, and then improvises the actual wording of the story in relation to the audience response. Thus no two tellings of an oral story are exactly alike, but they are similar. In his research on the nature of storytelling, Alfred Bates Lord discovered that across many story traditions, 90 per cent of an oral epic is assembled from lines repeated verbatim or with one-for-one word substitutions. Oral stories are built out of phrases—patterns—stockpiled from a lifetime of hearing and telling stories.

From all of this, quantities can be calculated and cost analysis and cost allocation processes derived. Further, the model can be used to simulate the performance of the building—its energy use, internal lighting, how people will move through the building and so on.

4D modelling applies to buildings, too, in exploring project phasing, scheduling and sequence planning, and in assisting construction site management, including the simulation of construction

Figure 3.20 Script and storyboard outline for animated movie *Obese Alice*. Courtesy of Jacob White.

As with other forms of design, a story is typically based on an established pattern. For both digital and traditional media, we refer to genres. Publishers understand genre and its potentially ready-made audience. Nadeane Trowse likens genres to games, with set rules, able to 'facilitate engagement with a social process' (2002: 341). Genre is a hierarchical construct, so that within a genre there are subgenres. In cinema, for example, mood, setting and format are often cited as interrelated components. Film theorist Barry Grant illustrates the key elements of genre in conventions, iconography, setting, types of stories and characters, stories and themes (2007). The emotional charge carried throughout the film is known as its mood. The film's location is its setting. The film's organization and style of scenes or shots is its format. In the mood sub-genre alone there are many types:

- **Action**—generally involves a moral interplay between good and bad played out through violence or physical force
- **Adventure**—involves danger, risk and/or chance, often with a high degree of fantasy
- **Comedy**—intended to provoke laughter
- **Drama**—mainly focuses on character development

- **Fantasy**—concerns speculative fiction outside reality (i.e. myth, legend)
- **Horror**—intended to provoke fear
- **Mystery**—involves the progression from the unknown to the known by discovering and solving a series of clues
- **Romance**—dwells on the elements of romantic love
- **Thrillers**—intended to provoke excitement and/or nervous tension

The rules of a conventional script-writing genre may be bent. In the portmanteau style, for example, a series of scenes is assembled according to a common idea, incident, sound or image. *New York Stories* used place, *Four Rooms* used a person and *Twenty Buck Coffee and Cigarettes* used a thing to bind the film elements together. The setting typically follows from the mood, although a director may change settings without changing mood or format, as with a Shakespeare play set in twentieth-century New York.

Rules of the three-act play

The most common format for film is the three-act play. A problem is posed for the hero in the first few minutes of a feature film. The problem may be a quest for love or fulfilment, a search for

Figure 3.21 *Legoland*, stills from animated movie.
Courtesy of Laura Le Blanc.

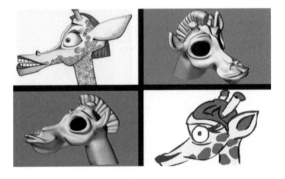

Figure 3.22 Character design for the main character,
Alice, a dietary-challenged performer in the short animation
Obese Alice. Courtesy of Jacob White.

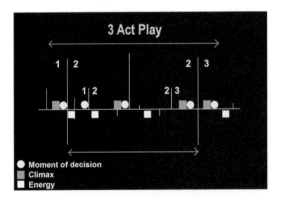

Figure 3.23 Typical three-act play graphic storyline action.
Courtesy of Dean Bruton.

something or a solution to a personal dilemma. Usually, the first act sets up this problem and introduces the hero/protagonist(s). The second act tests the hero/protagonist in a variety of ways, usually with a crescendo/climax just before the third act. The third act is about a resolution of the problem. Well-known plays from antiquity use a concept of scene, and this concept remains in software programs such as Adobe Flash, used for interactive stories. Any plot can be represented by a graph to show how the action develops in a pattern based on the genre and the context of the story.

These patterns of mood, setting and format guide the story line with characters (human or otherwise) and plot. Internal coherence is fundamental: all parts of a good story are there for a reason, mutually supporting the fabric of the communication. Each aspect of a character and the environment has been designed to develop the story.

The beginning idea is usually called a *concept* and can be expressed in one paragraph or even in one sentence. Most concepts are inevitably based on preexisting patterns, but brainstorming sessions try to move beyond the obvious choices. Describing desirable qualities for the product is often a good starting point for idea generation. This assists the concept development by providing a focus for the design of the components and their assembly. For example, desirable qualities of a potential script or project might be snappy, intriguing, original, flavoursome or marketable. This concept is developed as a plot.

Plots can be linear or nonlinear. Film is a linear medium because we get a repeat experience with each viewing. By contrast, interactive digital media is nonlinear because the user can redirect the story at any time. The digital designer manipulates the game player by planning each interaction carefully before the visual material is constructed. For games and movie production, the plot is usually outlined in a storyboard. Software such as *Final Draft* or *Movie Magic Screenwriter* (Craig 2012) offer predetermined patterns for organizing the storyboard instead of traditional methods of paper and pen.

Plot development

As the plot of a story develops, the elements of the changes are depicted in successive images until the entire story can be seen in a pictorial overview. This visual representation assists a design team to envision and share the plot, characters and narrative voice. The vocabulary and rules for the story are then easier to discern.

Typically, the following questions need to be answered in a storyboard:

Mood

Who is the principal character?
What is the character's age, sex, background?
What will happen to the character?
Will the character be changed by the course of the narrative?
Will the character have a distinct personality?
Or will she, he, or it be blank, to allow the player full control?

Setting

Where is the story set?
What is the environment?
What are the locations?

Figure 3.24 *Pet Rock,* still from short animation.
Courtesy of Tim Forbes and Jacob White.

Figure 3.25 Still from a television series using a rule-based design approach. Each episode was based on a phobia's name that began with a letter of the alphabet; *Figaro Pho*, 2010. Courtesy of Luke Jurevicius and Andrew Kunzel.

Format

How are the scenes organized?

What is the style of image?

In the following typical pattern for a drama plot or story, a nine-point plan adds detail to the traditional three-act model.

Designing the middle bit

In a movie, Scene 2 or Act 2 is always a challenge for the scriptwriter, who needs to devise second-act tests for the hero to overcome. These tests give clues about the character's personal qualities and allow the scriptwriter to fill in the back story. Ultimately the middle bit sets up for the viewer the opportunity for a full understanding of the impact of the final act and the resolution of all aspects of the story. A good movie character design usually takes this into account. For the design of an effective game character, the levels of each game need careful consideration. As the player progresses through each game level toward the game's con-

Table 3.1   STRUCTURE OF A THREE-ACT PLAY

	Nine-point plan	Three-act model
Normality	First act	
Disturbance	First act	
Protagonist	First act	The setup
Plan	First act	Actions in response to the disturbance
Surprise	First act	First-act turning point
Obstacle	First act	
	End of first act	
Complication, substories, more surprises and obstacles	Second and third acts	Second act, third act up to climax
	Climax	Climax
Resolution	End of third act	How the world goes on
	End of film	End of film

Figure 3.26 A grammatical approach to set design for a mobile phone game. Courtesy of James Pearse.

clusion, the well-designed character develops cohesive complexity and personal relevance.

Character design

In most movies and games, the main vocabulary elements are the (human or nonhuman) characters. Any character (fictional or nonfictional) has a potential back story, a series of events that shape the context of personality and behaviour. Characters can be aliens, animals, gods or, occasionally, inanimate objects. Characters are almost always at the centre of fictional texts, especially novels and plays. The extraordinarily popular *Harry Potter* series of novels written by J.K. Rowling and the film versions of the books demonstrate the power of good character design. Harry Potter is the hero at the centre of the action. By contrast, James Joyce's *Finnegan's Wake* is rare story without a character at the centre of the action.

The design process of characterization explores character types and motivations. Each character type has a set of rules for their actions. These actions can be derived from asking questions such as 'What does she or he look like?',

'How do they move?', 'Why does she, he or it do that?' and 'What kind of sounds do they make?' The considerations for the character's design in any story are to

- establish the primary agent's or primary character's goal, task and outlook;
- add secondary character(s) as foil, support, information and catalyst;
- build character's physical, mental and emotional contrasts; and
- introduce character(s)' obstacles and path diversions.

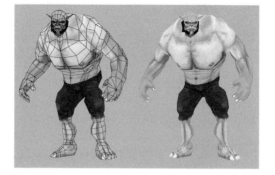

Figure 3.27 3D character design pose, low polygon setup for game animation. Courtesy of Andrew Osborne.

Archetypes

The journey and the goal are core archetypical elements that shape the narrative.

The Hero	The Journey	The Goal
Orphan	Questing	Self-Worth
Magician	Initiation	Knowledge
Warrior	Adventure	Justice

As usual in design, the notions of archetypes and stereotypes—well-defined patterns—assist the definition of a character's role.

Characterization can involve developing a variety of aspects of a character, such as appearance, age, gender, educational level, vocation or occupation, financial status, marital status, social status, hobbies, religious beliefs, ambitions and motivations. The psychological makeup of a fully developed storybook character may involve fears, emotions, backstory, issues, beliefs, practices, desires and intentions. These can be shown through the actions and language of the character, rather than by telling the audience directly.

Often, fictional characters are different from and have different beliefs than the author. A writer of fiction can assume the point of view of a child, an older person, a member of the opposite gender or someone of another personality, race or culture. The story teller might be a character manifest as a narrative voice. Digital design offers a variety of open source and commercial software to assist, including many plug-ins for facial animation, the development of lip-sync for voice control and even script writing and production programs to enable the construction of these character design qualities within the story line.

Digital places

Digital stories, of course, contain both objects and places. In the stories discussed above, the experience is predetermined, controlled by the director/designer. The kind of digital place we want to focus on here is one that allows exploration, where the audience has control of the route

Figure 3.28 Character design involves intense exploration of a variety of forms. Courtesy of Jacob White.

through space and the selection of experiences along the way. Many of the issues in designing digital places are the same as those in designing physical spaces: identity, consistency, legibility, ease of circulation and avoiding the disconcerting visitor experience of being lost in a place with insufficient signposting. Thinking about the grammar for a virtual world is like thinking about the grammar for an object or story: what are the vocabulary elements and what are the rules by which they are linked?

A good Web site design typically has an economical vocabulary and rule set. Consider the grammar of Google and how the designers of this Web site have rigorously resisted the temptation to add more vocabulary elements or complicate the rules of interaction. Even the energy-efficient Blackle site adheres to these rules (black because a black screen uses less energy than a white screen). Web site design rules, patterns, schemas and templates are available online, and standard software offerings in Adobe Flash, Microsoft Word and other programs allow the novice to quickly create a Web site without having to understand the mechanics of the design. Rule books and guidelines for designing Web sites abound, so there are many canons that beg to be bent or broken.

The typical Web site presents a two-dimensional environment. A virtual world is a computer-based simulated three-dimensional environment intended for its users to inhabit and interact via avatars. This habitation is commonly realized in the form of two- or three-dimensional graphical representations of humanoids (or other graphical or text-based avatars).

Some, but not all, virtual worlds allow for multiple users. The rule sets and patterns of virtual worlds are frequently modelled on those of the

Figure 3.29 Buildings constructed from a vocabulary of modular elements for game environments. Courtesy of Alexander Brazier.

Character Typology

Typical character types include:

- Hero or Antihero
- Mentor or Ally
- Catalyst
- Victim
- Sage
- Clown

familiar physical world. Consider Second Life and its music and arts festival Secondfest (in 2007 for the first time ever Secondfest brought a festival experience to Second Life).

The vocabulary and rule set of the event and the vocabulary and rule set of the place are both drawn from real-world established patterns, with

Figure 3.30 Set design for short animation showing the addition of photographic mapping and lighting to the model. Courtesy of Jacob White.

Figure 3.31 Web folio concept design, blocking out text and multimedia elements. Courtesy of James Burroughs.

virtual sound stages and dance tents and also a camp site with showers and portable toilets.

This approach to virtual worlds allows us to transfer our accumulated store of behaviour patterns and recognition of environmental patterns from the real world into the virtual world. If that was not the case, it would be like being born again and having to learn anew how to operate within the social structures of life.

Digital games

The writer's control of the plot in a book or film largely directs the viewer's experience although much still relies on an individual's interpretation. The writer for a game design must decide on the extent to which the player can manipulate the story. The trick is to give the player the illusion of full control. Players like to feel that their input directs the story, but in reality, the programmed game has a finite number of sequences, and the player is merely choosing one of those available. 'Formed by rules and experienced through play, a game is a space of possible action that players activate, manipulate, explore and transform' (Salen and Zimmerman 2004: 378).

In discussing the nature of interactive storytelling, 'language equals vocabulary plus grammar'

(2005: 169). If we ignore the environment, the vocabulary and rule set of a game are obvious: the
vocabulary of objects, including those controlled
by the player, and the rules by which the objects
are allowed to interact. In the classic game of
Pong (also called ping-pong), the environment is
an empty screen, the vocabulary is two bats and
a ball, and the rules govern the way that the ball
is reflected off the bats and how the bats and ball
can move. The history of digital games shows a
return to these fundamentals whilst incorporating
the rapid development of new technologies that
enrich the gaming experience. If we regard the
bats and balls in *Pong* as characters, their design is straightforward and their range of actions
well defined and predictable according to easily
understood rules. In more complex games with
human-like characters, the game play also partly
depends on the rules for the character(s)' design
and animation.

First-person shooter video games position the
player as a weapon-wielding action-avatar moving through a virtual environment populated by
beings that try to terminate the player. This is a
common genre, often with strong combat and
violence elements. The weapons typically exem-
plify the consistent vocabulary and defined rules
in the game. Each weapon has a set of rules for
its operation.

In the game *Resistance: Fall of Man*, the Chi-
mera characters illustrate the way the metaphor
of evil can permeate a nemesis character design.
Originally humans, they have mutated. They are
stronger than humans physically and have a me-
tabolism twelve times that of the average human,
so they can regenerate and are exceedingly agile.
They have bright orange eyes, with some having
two and some having six. More of this species
are produced when the Chimeran parasite enters

Figure 3.32 Serious game design: using a game engine
for the serious training of mine workers. Courtesy of James
Pearse.

Interaction with Avatars

Character design can shape the action of the story and have
a powerful impact on the way a game player is able to see
possible game play paths. Designing characters requires
consideration of the rules for their appearance and behaviour. Characters in an interactive environment behave differently than those in linear media (Miller 2004). A character's
appearance is often associated with their role.

a human body. The premise of human origin allows the character designer to adopt many of the
vocabulary elements and rules of a human, but
these are crossed with vocabularies and rules
from insect and crustacean worlds.

A user's communication with the game design
vocabulary and rules is managed by an interface.
This can be as simple as a chess board or as
complex as a flight deck simulator. The layout,
the formal visual qualities and the protocols of the
interactive process determine the richness of the
user interaction. New approaches to interface
design include rules that are contingent. For example, the simulation engine Euphoria simulates

Figure 3.33 Action in a computer game proposal,
Tillian Tribes. Courtesy of James Pearse.

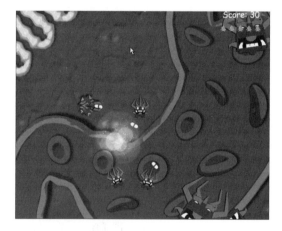

Figure 3.34 Cell phone game concept: fighting disease.
Courtesy of James Pearse.

the unpredictability of real life, enabling 'interactive characters to move, act and even think like actual human beings, adapting their behaviour on the fly and resulting in a different payoff every single time' (LucasArts 2007). The action is not scripted but simulated, with contingencies in the game so that players will never be able to predict exactly what will happen, no matter how many times they have experienced a certain scenario.

Serious games enlist the enjoyment and immersion of digital games to prepare people to respond to comparable real-life situations, most obviously in the military and emergency services but extending to the management of processes and equipment. Unlike a conventional manual, a game presents diverse and unexpected situations and lets trainees develop their skills in how to react.

In the next chapter we turn our attention to the question of creativity.

Summary: Commonalities

In this chapter we have investigated how a focus on rules and contingency applies in several design subfields. We find the same basic concepts in all of them.

chapter 4

developing digital creativity

Are there ways to increase our creativity in digital design? We all want to be creative, but what does it mean? Creativity relates to creation, to creating some thing or idea or action. The same themes recur in every field of endeavour— we can recognize the same qualities.

can we be more creative with digital design?

Whatever the field, creativity is evident in four ways: in the creative product, the creative process, the creative person and the creative situation (Briskman 1981; Brown 1989). The creative person in a creative situation follows a creative process to produce creative products (e.g. ideas, insights, designs, art). The key is the outcome—people, processes and places are only deemed to be creative if the products are deemed to be creative.

Defining creativity

Definitions of a creative product typically link novelty with acceptability (Torrance 1977). Judgements of both novelty and acceptability (where acceptability can be regarded as an expression of value) are subject to time and to cultural and personal variation, so judgements of creativity are never absolute. Indeed, creative ideas and products are often rejected because they are too far outside the norm, defying the consensus on what is appropriate (Csikszentmihalyi 1988). Time and again, initial critical reviews of what are later considered to be major artistic works are negative, even damning (Sternberg and Lubart 1996). This is not an acknowledged conservatism; rather, it is the unconscious reinforcement of the status quo, the group knowledge about a field.[1]

Only later does the group come to realize that the creative act was indeed both new and valuable, and assimilates it into its understanding of the field. This also means that immediate, universal applause for an artwork or idea is often a sign that it is not, actually, particularly creative (Sternberg 2006).

ways to be creative

Being creative and doing creative things is a question of degree, not just presence or absence.[2] Life is ceaselessly creative, both at the grand level of evolution and the small level of our own human life. There are several ways in which a person or product can be seen to be creative (Sternberg 2006: 96, citing Gardner 1993).

1. **Type of creativity that accepts current paradigms and extends them.** In this type, the patterns are refined, replicated or incrementally advanced, but with no significant challenge to the existing rules of design or behaviour. This type of creativity is the most common response to contingency. We can see it in work that rides the current wave of digital design trends and adds to the wave by extending its power and scope.

Figure 4.1 A digitally designed portrait of his shaggy dog, Harry, for a short animation. Courtesy of Tim Forbes.

2. **Type of creativity that rejects current paradigms and replaces them.** In this type, the current patterns and rules are abandoned and new ones adopted—new ones that may be drawn from earlier paradigms. We can see it in work that seems to start a new wave heading in a new direction, even if the new wave is drawn from the depths of history. This type of creativity is rare.

Creation of the Google Search Engine

In 1997 Larry Page and Sergey Brin decided that their BackRub search engine needed a new name. After some brainstorming, they went with Google—a play on the word 'googol', a mathematical term for the number represented by the numeral 1 followed by 100 zeros. The use of the term reflected their mission to organize a seemingly infinite amount of information on the Web.

3. **Type of creativity that links and synthesizes current paradigms.** In this type, two or more formerly disconnected sets of patterns and rules, including patterns of thinking, are integrated. We can see this type when ideas from one field are used in another field.

We could investigate the question of creativity in digital design through the nature of the created product, or through the nature of the process, the person or the situation. Here we will explore all these approaches in turn.

We begin by looking at what constitutes a creative product because we cannot really describe creative processes, people and situations without reference to the products that result.

the creative product

A product is not deemed creative because it is an exemplary instance of the ordinary—the perfectly made digital dog that is much the same as other digital dogs. Such perfection in the use of established rules may be praised as craftsmanship and professionalism, but not as creative work. So creativity is judged by evaluating a product in relation to what has become normal in the relevant field. If the digital dog is different in some way—personality, appearance, expression—then others might see it as creative. In design and art an understanding of the rules, pattern(s) and grammar(s) of the background is a precondition to both making and recognizing surprising innovations. A surprising outcome is surprising because it lies outside what is expected from the rule system, and may even cause a radical reframing of our understanding of the rule system. 'One of the paradoxes of

Figure 4.2 Instances of biomorphic forms designed with the generative software *Origine*, 2009. Courtesy of Dean Bruton.

creativity is that, in order to think originally, we must familiarise ourselves with the ideas of others . . . These ideas can then form a springboard from which the creator's ideas can be launched' (Kneller 1965, qtd in Lawson 1980: 118).

How do we know what is standard? Merely being presented with product examples is not enough. We need to begin to understand their design languages, vocabularies and rules. Innovation comes from understanding the limits of tradition and breaking through those limits. 'Tradition, rather than being the stifling set of rules and structures it is sometimes supposed to be, may be precisely the condition through which genuine innovation is possible' (Freeman 1993: 210).

The springboard to creativity is not necessarily constructed from exceptional products. Robert Venturi explains that the extraordinary can be derived from the ordinary:

Convention is something we are not afraid of—we like it, we embrace it . . . We love the ordinary, we make the ordinary extraordinary. We learnt a lot from Pop artists [e.g. Andy Warhol] who did the *Campbell soup can* and gave it another context and another scale and it became extra ordinary. So convention, again; we love looking out of a window of a train or a car and we just learn all the time from the every day. I think that is different from the heroic stance of, 'I don't learn from the ordinary I despise the ordinary'—my job is to be extraordinary. I think that it is true—good art is extraordinary, but it can be derived from the ordinary. There is a long tradition of that. (Venturi and Scott-Brown 1996)

The very fact that the audience, the judge of creativity, is very familiar with the rules of the ordinary makes it more likely that bent and broken rules will

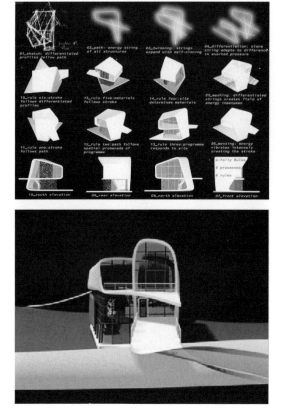

Figure 4.3 Taking a pattern from calligraphy and using it in architecture: the grid illustrates the development of a building design from calligraphic mark to final form, *Stroke House*, 2003. Courtesy of Kent Neo.

be recognized and the product extolled as creative (if it can overcome the acceptability barrier, noted previously, that can lead to the thoughtless rejection of creative outcomes).

Novelty may simply extend the existing background (the first type of creativity listed) or (and more interestingly) may actually conflict with this background or necessitate its modification (the second type of creativity listed). 'In fact', Briskman writes,

it seems to me that when we are thinking of really great creative achievements (especially in science, although similar considerations can, I

think, be applied to certain aspects of art) we are in the main thinking of this latter case . . . [R]eally outstanding creative achievements have a habit of breaking, in important ways, with the tradition out of which they emerged. They, so to speak, transcend this tradition. (1981: 96)

In digital design (as in art), the value of uniqueness resulting from commercialization has led to the characteristic of novelty being fore-fronted as the preeminent criterion of quality. Novelty is easy: anyone can make something that is different for difference's sake (Bentley 1999). What is difficult is to combine novelty with true value, where value includes aesthetic and functional aspects. The novelty of a creative artwork will reinterpret its subject in ways that are not only different but also respond to an audience's changed attitudes and expectations. It will respond to the contingency of time. The novelty of an applied design will respond to a new function, a new constraint or a new demand. It will respond to the contingency of the environment in which the design is situated.

The natural world provides innumerable examples of the rich and productive possibilities contingency prompts. We can witness, for example, the enormous beauty in diversity of a coral reef. We have learnt about the variations in the structure of DNA molecules and their arrangements for the formation of life. The creativity of nature responds to the contingency of nature.

the creative process

If we accept that creativity exists in several ways and at many levels, the most common creative process is associated with the first type listed previously (creativity that accepts current para-digms and extends them). We highlight the small extension or adaptation of the rules and patterns of accepted paradigms in response to contin-gency. How far this process is prepared to stray from the safety of current paradigms is an indica-tion of the degree of creativity involved.

Briskman clarifies the value of thinking the un-thinkable: 'Moreover, insofar as creative products actually conflict with the tradition out of which they emerge, insofar as they are prohibited by that tra-dition, creative thinking actually involves the think-ing of *forbidden thoughts*' (1981: 96).[3]

The thinking of 'forbidden thoughts' refers to the way in which expectations of product form are so deeply imbedded in our thinking (our fore-understanding in the terms of the hermeneutic cir-cle) that going outside of these expectations is not even considered—or seen as abnormal or anti-authority. Forbidden thoughts instigate disruption, a linked concept that we will return to later.

Standard thought takes place within a particu-lar framing of a situation, and although we operate within many such frames, we only do so one at a time. Arthur Koestler argued that the creative act

> combines, reshuffles, and relates already exist-
> ing but hitherto separate ideas, facts, frames
> of perception, associative contexts. This act
> of cross-fertilization—or self-fertilization within
> a single brain—seems to be the essence of
> creativity. (1981: 2)

Koestler emphasizes association of ideas, see-ing creativity as the coming together of two old ideas to make a single appropriate and novel idea.[4] He called this crossing between and relat-ing two normally independent frames of reference a 'bisociation of matrices' (1964: 2). The re-use

Designing a Generative Visual Experience

Examples of digital design that use the contingency of na-ture are seen in the generative design of Casey Reas and Tal Rosner. In 2011 they collaborated on a site-specific video mural for the new Frank Gehry–designed home of the New World Symphony in Miami. Custom-written software not only creates hourly cycles of imagery, but it generates an ever-changing visual experience over time for new and repeat visitors, regardless of the time, the day or the season.

Figure 4.4 Screen stills form the installation by Casey Reas and Tal Rosner on the Frank Gehry–designed home of the New World Symphony in Miami. Courtesy of Casey Reas and Tal Rosner.

of a well-known pattern is unlikely to be regarded as highly creative. Similarly, only following es-tablished rules is not a route to high creativity in digital design. But taking a pattern from one field

Figure 4.5 Iterative rule application for development of virtual form. Courtesy of Doudou Huang.

and applying it in another, quite different, field is a much-followed path in the third kind of creativity listed at the beginning of this chapter.[5]

Lateral and divergent thinking and brainstorming techniques break down the normal barriers between frames. Building on J. P. Guilford's work, E. Paul Torrance (1977) defined creativity as a testable ability in divergent thinking with five dimensions (fluency, originality, elaboration, abstractness of titles and resistance to premature closure). The literature on creativity offers a wealth of thinking techniques and tips by authors such as James Adams (1990), De Bono (2007), Michalko (2001) and Hurson (2008).

creativity and rules

Producing variants entirely within a preexisting rule set is likely to be seen as mechanistic and not creative. This would apply whether or not the rules are encoded in a computer system. Yet we have noted that rules are interpreted and used contingently to suit specific situations; it is how they are used that matters. We are prepared to assign the adjective 'creative' to a musical performance because of the way the performer interprets the rules of the score. Harrison argues that in music 'the difference between a good and very bad performance cannot be spelt out in the score and . . . hence such a score is not a recipe for the repetition of a certain result since the playing of music is an art form, the creativity the flair of the player' and asserts that 'no recipe can itself contain instructions for how it should be followed' (1978: 71).

If we accept a narrow view of the incompatibility of creativity and mechanism, the creative act requires one of two components in relation to rules: adding to the rules, or breaking the rules (thinking 'forbidden thoughts'). Garry Stewart (2010), artistic director of the Australian Dance

Theatre, claims that 'we decide what the rules are, for ourselves'. Most breaks or interventions will be discarded in evaluation, while a few may be retained in a continually evolving grammar—akin to Darwinian evolution.

There are several important points to make here. The first is that since during the practice of digital design and art, rules are frequently being broken and recast, this necessary criterion for creativity is regularly met.

The second point is that the rule set is only a part of a design tradition. The continuing inter-action of this part with others is the reason for the importance of contingency in the way that we look at and apply the whole notion of a set of rules.

Thirdly, this way of looking at creativity accords with our assertion that instances of change in vo-cabularies and rules during the derivation of a de-sign (of breaking and recasting rules) corresponds with moments of inspiration—the most creative moments.

It is said that necessity is the mother of inven-tion. It is difficult to disrupt our familiar thought processes unless we are forced to do so. We tend to be most creative when we are forced to frame the situation in new ways, to try new pat-terns and bend the rules, because the usual way

Figure 4.7 Stages in the development of a design for a fan. Courtesy of Doudou Huang.

will not work. Indeed, if these problems do not arise naturally, it can help to force them, to work as if the obvious approaches were not allowed. For example, Apple has consistently adhered to a pattern of disruption of traditional digital design thinking. Many of the products of this company challenge the ideas that were held by its counter-parts and tradition.

the creative person

'The innovative person must dare to differ, make changes, stand out, challenge traditions, make

Figure 4.6 Instances of virtual wheel hubs generated by parametric modelling with Genoform. Courtesy of Genometri Ltd.

a few waves and bend a few rules' (Davis 1983: 37).[6] Preempting Gary Davis's classic work, Sidney Parnes (1967) ascribed the following characteristics to creative people[7]:

> Conceptual fluency
>
> Originality
>
> Determination
>
> Task-oriented/problem-focused behaviour
>
> Willingness to suspend judgment
>
> Relativist (rather than determinist) outlook
>
> Independence
>
> Imagination
>
> Playfulness
>
> Tolerance of ambiguity

Without attributing these qualities to nature or nurture categories, it is important to say that they are honed by disciplined practice. John Hayes, noting that there is wide agreement among researchers that preparation is important for creativity, surveyed 76 great composers and 131 great painters:

> The pattern of career productivity for these painters was similar to that observed in the composers. There was an initial period of non-creativity lasting about six years. This was followed by a rapid increase in productivity over the next six years, then a period of stable productivity until about 35 years into their careers, and lastly a period of declining productivity. Wishbow (1988) conducted a biographical study . . . of 66 eminent poets . . . She found that none of her 66 poets wrote a notable poem earlier than five years into their careers, and 55 of the 66 poets produced none earlier than 10 years into their careers. (1989: 139)[8]

Experts read situations by recognizing patterns (Lawson 1980). Referring to research by Simon and Chase (1973) suggesting that chess players needed about ten years of preparation and to 'learn a vast store' of around 50,000 chess patterns in order to play the game at the grand master level, Hayes observes, 'One can easily imagine that composers, painters, and poets need a comparable time to acquire sufficient knowledge and skills to perform in their fields at world class levels' (1989: 140). Freeman in his study of artists interviewed several who refer to the patterns of art:

> Art, she came to believe, rather than being some divine gift from above, was instead a learnable skill, having to do with 'our basic drive to find patterns and likenesses around us.' She also came to believe that it was important for people, her students especially, to see art in these terms. But if they were anything like she herself had been, there would have to be a good deal of demythologising for this to be possible. (1993: 75)

With respect to the digital designer's need for preparation, we have argued already that the recognition of the importance of 'patterns and likenesses' and the ability to draw on a 'vast store' of such patterns and contingently apply them is an essential part of creative activity. This informs and challenges design thinking for new work.[9]

knowledge versus creativity

Can knowledge be a two-edged sword? Knowledge about a field can lead to a narrow understanding of what is possible, and inhibit risk taking. For example, a photographer referred to her early work as being more creative than her later, more refined, work. In the early photographs she did not know 'what she should not do'.

In the same way that evolutionary biologists think that a new species does not arise without some degree of isolation, it has been argued that radically new ideas and designs may require isolation from dominant paradigms (Harford 2010).[10]

Yet, in investigating the tension between knowledge and creativity, Robert Weisberg hypothesizes that 'one will never find an individual who has made a significant contribution to a creative discipline without having first deep initial immersion in that discipline' (1999: 242).

Where someone appears to come from outside to make a breakthrough in an area, what seems to be happening is that this person sees the situation as one familiar in his or her own area in which the person does have this background of deep immersion.

Adopting terms that are compatible with Rorty's work, we can think of the grammar a digital designer, artist (or composer or poet) customarily uses as embracing a personal vocabulary, a personal way of doing things. Rorty comments that 'all we can do is work with the final vocabulary we have, while keeping our ears open for hints about how it might be expanded or revised' (1989: 197).

Self-creation, identity, and understanding of one's legitimate place in a community are all aspects of design endeavour. Barbara Herrnstein Smith suggests that artists and designers judge their work 'by articulating an estimate of how well that work will serve certain implicitly defined functions' (1988: 13). This relates to the digital designer's iterative task of finding a voice, a personal expression within his or her folio and life's work.

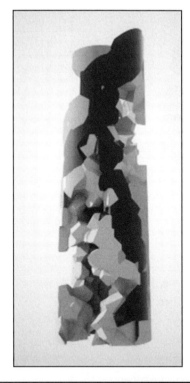

Figure 4.8 Two views of a skyscraper design competition entry, 2010. Courtesy of Xiong Lu.

We make the following additions to Parnes's list of a successful designer's personal qualities. The successful creative digital designer is

acutely aware of the wealth of patterns that the world offers;

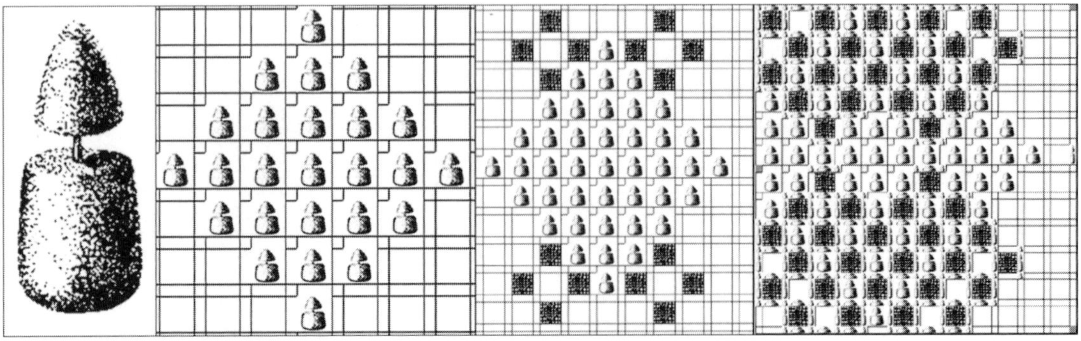

Figure 4.9 The iterative application of replacement rules generates patterns on a tartan grid with the software program *Tartan Worlds* developed by Paul Taplin. Courtesy of Dean Bruton.

able to recognize the vocabularies and rules in the phenomena of both natural and designed worlds;

confident in the ability to respond to contingency by adapting patterns and rule sets, but not easily satisfied;

willing to take dangerous or contentious risks in bending and breaking rules; willing to respond to criticism by bending rules in unexpected ways; and

passionate about designing.

Motivation is central. People rarely do truly creative work unless they love what they are doing and focus on the doing rather than the potential rewards (Amabile 1983, cited in Sternberg 2006). Creative giants tend to give up many of the common pleasures of life in exchange for outstanding success in their creative work (Gardner 1993).[11]

the creative situation

Archimedes famously had a moment of inspiration in his bath, some of us have our best thoughts under our showers, architect Keith Cottier referred to designing an award-winning Australian building while hiking in the Austrian mountains and many of the most constructive and brilliant ideas seem to come together in group discussion late at night over coffee or a bottle of wine—although the ideas that seem so brilliant at the time can be elusive the following morning.

In the next chapter we describe a grammar for the Cylinda-Line range of tableware manufactured in Denmark since the 1960s. In a brochure marking the 100-year anniversary of its designer Arne Jacobsen's birth, its manufacturer Stelton described its creation by a busy and reluctant architect.

During a dinner party—almost as if saying 'The hell with it'—Jacobsen sketched a few cylindrical forms on his napkin. This is how the range should look: terse, logical and functional. (Stelton 2002: 16)

The common pattern in these creative situations is the experience of relaxation and well-being after a long period of thought and reflection, either or both about the specific design task or about languages of design in general. Stressful situations are not creative situations—although

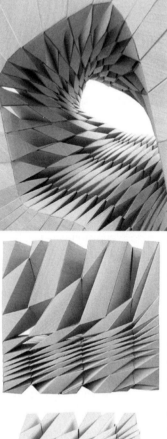

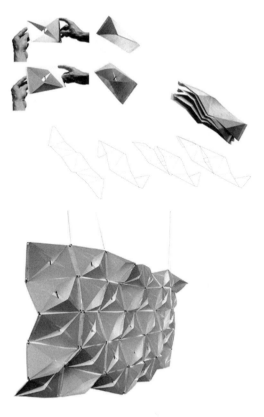

Figure 4.11 *In-Out Curtain*, designed by IwamotoScott, is a prototype for a hybrid drape/venetian blind that combines modular origami and digital production. Each module is made up of cut, perforated, folded, and interlocked laser-cut sheets. Adjusted by hand, modules can be either in or out but are interlinked so that they work together as an operable screen. Courtesy of Lisa Iwamoto (2009: 76, 77 and http://www.iwamotoscott.com, accessed 1 June 2011).

Figure 4.10 A 'rest box' designed by IwamotoScott for the 2010 Gwangju Design Biennale in South Korea 'takes atmospheric elements made from primary materials of the garden including the filtered light of trees, shadow patterns of jagged stone, and striated shadows from trunks. These are re-made in the box using folded hollow blocks made from laminated wood veneer . . . An interior void is "carved" through the box to create a space of rest, which accommodates a body in a range of positions, from sitting to reclining.' Courtesy of Lisa Iwamoto, http://www. iwamotoscott.com, accessed 1 June 2011.

History of Multiplayer Environments

The creation of massive multiplayer games (MMPs) is a major part of the development of digital culture: a situation where reality and virtuality merge.

Multiplayer games are a specific genre of online games, featuring thousands of players playing simultaneously on a persistent world map. Players create alter egos (as avatars) in these worlds and guide them as they grow more powerful.

In 1997 Electronic Arts launched *Ultima Online*, which redefined the market and boasts over 200,000 subscribers. In 1999 Sony Online Entertainment launched *EverQuest* in competition, beating the Microsoft/Turbine title *Asheron's Call* to market. By 2012 it had around 5 million subscribers. Other successes include Mythic Entertainments' *Dark Age of Camelot*, launched in 2002. Well-known examples include *Matrix Online*, *Lord of the Rings Online*, *EverQuest 2*, *World of Warcraft*, *UO Odyssey* and *City of Heroes*.

perhaps necessity is the mother of invention, the design engineered under stress tends to the pragmatic rather than the conceptually or physically beautiful.

How, then, can the situation in what we might call a grammatical studio engender a creative situation?

The answer follows directly from the themes we have already explored. The grammatical studio will promote constructive thought and reflection-in-action on the grammatical possibilities that might exist in any design context—through the grammars of precedents, through the grammars imbedded in design media, and above all through self-awareness of the artist or designer's own grammatical development.

Then the grammatical studio will promote an experience of enjoyment and well-being through a sense of play and engagement. A grammatical studio is a place where artists and designers want to be.

But there must still be an edge; it should not be too comfortable, a place of passive predictability and minimal effort. The grammatical studio is a place where digital designers make each other and themselves nervous by playing at the edge of the familiar, taking risks and uncomfortably—but excitingly—disrupting conventions and expectations. Architect Frank Gehry explains:

> For me, every day is new thing. I approach each project with a new insecurity, almost like the first project I ever did. And I get the sweats. I go in and start working, I'm not sure where I'm going. If I knew where I was going I wouldn't do it. When I can predict or plan it, I don't do it. I discard it. So I approach it with the same trepidation. (2002)

The most important aspect of a creative digital environment is peer support. In an environment where people are too ready to criticize, to point out problems, the individual will play safe. The group as well as the individual needs to take risks.

For the digital designer working in physical isolation, a sheltered online community akin to that of a multiplayer game environment might be a viable alternative. The sharing of digital design journals or blogs can also enable members of a group to support each other.

disruption

How can a digital designer incorporate radical shifts in his or her work, going off the edge of the languages that a grammar implicitly defines, thinking forbidden thoughts and disrupting expectations?

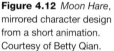

Figure 4.12 *Moon Hare*, mirrored character design from a short animation. Courtesy of Betty Qian.

Consider Edward Lucie-Smith's cool assessment of success in mainstream art. Being a first-rate follower of existing rule sets is not enough. Success for an artist, he suggests, requires an obvious manifestation of creativity through the disruption of existing rule sets. It requires the construction of unexpected, and hence fresh and challenging, apparently new rule sets. But commercial and critical success also requires a context in which such disruption is recognized and lauded, a privileged environment in which to make a mark.[12] He observes,

> There is a structural hierarchy in the operations of the international art world which centres on the bright stars in the constellation, the few artists, galleries, etc. who are 'on top' this decade. No matter how naturally part of the New York art world they might feel, however personally humble they might be as individuals, they remain the ones who define what currently defines art

in the culture. In so doing, they become the only artists with the chance to project their work into the long-term history of art. What gives them these powers is their exemplification of one simple, fundamental law within the rule-governed activity which art-making is: whereas most artists are rule following, these are both rule following and rule generating creators. They propose ways of making art which 'falsify' given ways, they satisfy doubts about these given ways, and they generate new problem areas for other artists to explore. Above all, they are in a situation which is culturally privileged for making their moves count. (1984: 51)

Disruption is the precursor to radical rethinking of grammar in architecture, too. Venturi and Denise Scott Brown, discussing their well-recorded process of planning and prototype production of the Philadelphia Orchestra Hall, were well aware of the changes in direction and moments of inspiration that occurred throughout their careers. Scott Brown reflects:

> But it was to kind of 'break the grammar'—to find a new one. And this was in the sixties in America where we said, 'We think social movements need to change in sensibilities, and then when sensibilities change, and our little thing can happen, catch your eye and make you realise a new grammar.' I think that's what happened with us. And that was what caught our eye to Las Vegas and began to give us a new set of forms, a new view of decoration and finally a realisation that symbolism was an important part of architecture. As we started to analyse what was it there that caught our eye and gave us a shiver. It wasn't even that we loved it. We don't know if we hated it or loved it, but it caused something to change. It helped us—it jolted our aesthetic—got us out of a rut and into a new way of thinking. We had a marvellous time in those days, Bob and I, playing a game, which said, 'I can like something worse than you can like', which was again: challenging your own grammars, saying, 'Now we're doing the 1950s'. All that terrible stuff that we hated in the 1950s, perhaps it's good. (Venturi and Scott-Brown 1996)

We argue in this chapter and throughout the book that fore-fronting rules (and associated concepts) in the way artists and designers think about their work sets up a way of thinking that has synergy with the intrinsic nature of computers.

> Computers will open new languages—new means of expression—not before possible or even conceivable. Computers will enable new worlds, new realities. We must have open eyes and open ears, open minds, if we are to appreciate these new worlds. We must develop a new aesthetic, a digital aesthetic. (Holtzman 1994: 252)

Many of the outcomes of digital design suggest an aesthetic more aligned with nature. Nicholas Grimshaw, architect of the Eden Project biosphere in the west of England, said,

> Technology and the growth of computers allow you a much freer palette as an architect.

Figure 4.13 Personal folio design inventively incorporating a community-based Web site for film and gaming enthusiasts. Courtesy of James Burroughs.

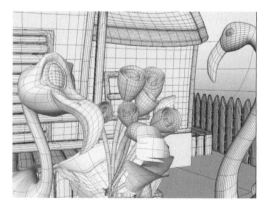

Figure 4.14 *Flamingos*, wire frame render of a still from the animated movie. Courtesy of Lisa Japp.

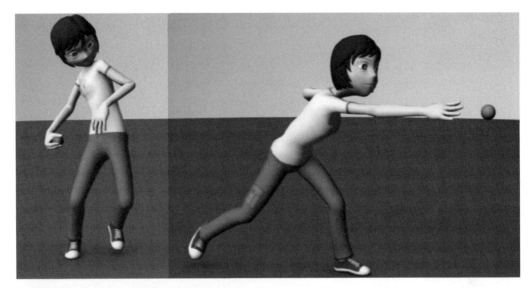

Figure 4.15 Principles of animation used in stills from a character throwing a ball. Courtesy of Lisa Japp.

Figure 4.16 *Spacestation*, image showing the importance of lighting a virtual space to enhance the dramatic mood. Courtesy of Claire Kearton.

Figure 4.17 *Can you please?*, music video, variations of a bear, 2010. Courtesy of Tom Lindley Donaldson and Tom Oates.

Also, the study of nature and the way plants grow is more and more available. Bring these things together and there is quite a strong human response. Combine with a better understanding of materials, [and] then we are in for a much richer phase of architecture. (1998)

Predictions of the future tend to look quaint when the future arrives, all too obviously imagined within the boundaries of the languages and expectations of the time of their making. As Albert Einstein is said to have commented, 'No problem can be solved by the same consciousness that created it. We need to see the world anew.'

We are not helpless in this enterprise. Sternberg (2006) tells us that to be creative we must first decide to generate new ideas, analyse these ideas and sell the ideas to others. We have to decide not to just follow other peoples' ideas, but rather to look for new patterns and make our own rules rather than just use the common ones, to get very good at recognizing what has potential

and throwing out the junk. This is what is meant by deciding to use our skills creatively, not looking for a creativity switch or passively waiting for our muse to inspire us.

One of the points we have emphasized in this chapter is the need to understand the past as a springboard for a creative future. In the next two chapters, we will analyse some examples of past digital and pre-digital design work that offer lessons for the future.

Summary

We have framed creativity within reflective practice and argued that a developed awareness of these concepts provides both an impetus and foundation for creativity. We locate disruption as the overturning and radical reframing of established patterns, vocabularies and rule sets. The creative act is closely associated with bending and occasionally breaking the rules, a response to the contingency of immediate contexts.

chapter 5

analysis: product design and art

In this chapter we turn our attention to analysing how, given a body of existing creative work, we can make a credible explanation of the vocabularies and rules that might underlie that work.

how do rules and contingency interplay in the work of celebrated designers and artists?

In analysing designs, we do not claim, nor need to claim, that 'this was how the designer did it.' Rather, we are interested in highlighting aspects of the work that can be precedents for our own digital design. These aspects typically have to do with the ways vocabulary and rules are used and adapted, not with the particular vocabulary and rules that we find.

In this chapter, we will discuss some examples from product design and art that show how rules and contingency interplay in the work of celebrated designers and artists. In the next chapter we will turn our attention to architecture, film and games. Some examples predate digital design but illustrate ideas with particular clarity. What we describe in these examples is the result of our own, or our cited sources', interpretations.

analysis and interpretation

The process of analysing the patterns and grammar(s) of a design typically follows the following sequence:

1. We identify the work or body of work of interest. This may be work which appears grammatical, but it may be the opposite—work chosen because it represents a challenge to the claim for universality of grammatical concepts. If it is a body of work, we can add or discard examples as the analysis progresses. Is the work an instance of a broader pattern?

2. We look for an underlying vocabulary: elements, shapes, materials, colours. This first attempt may be modified later.

3. We look for recurring patterns: assemblies, modifications to shapes and the ways materials are worked and combined. These recurring patterns disclose the rules because the rule is the way in which the pattern could have been created. As the analysis develops, new patterns are discovered and, equally, what at first may seem to be an important recurring pattern may turn out to be merely a side product of other, more basic patterns.

4. We can test our analysis by considering how the rules and patterns might be applied in making new designs and seeing if the results do appear to be credible members of the corpus of work.

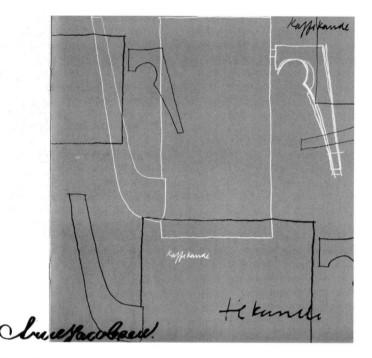

Figure 5.1 Sketch design for tableware by Arne Jacobsen, 1964. Courtesy of Stelton.

This, then, is a creative process in itself, in which the attempt to convincingly analyse the design leads to greater understanding and the possibility of improving the way the analysis is presented. Improving, in this context, can mean some combination of more credible, more elegant (explaining the derivation of designs with simpler and more easily understood rules, vocabularies and patterns), more general (encompassing a larger corpus of works) and more complete (accounting for more facets of the work) efforts. Early ways of looking at the work may be replaced by later, more productive, ways.[1] Ulrich Flemming, in a review of papers on computational grammatical approaches to art, concluded that

the experiences reported by these authors are similar to my own experiences with rule-based systems used by me as experimental tools to arrive at a deeper understanding of the compositional principles underlying certain corpora of architectural designs. My reaction too, was that the construction of an effective set of rules through a series of experiments was a creative process with its own rewards. (1996: 242–3)

Terry Knight, writer of many formal shape and colour grammars (much more precise than the kinds of analyses we seek here), describes the experience well. Despite her aim in writing a grammar to 'look at the works in an as unbiased way as possible,' she readily acknowledges that 'the grammar becomes the grammar writer's own theory of what is going on' (1996). Nevertheless, we can speculate on what contingencies led to changes in the rules and vocabularies.

Plate 1 *Komposition with Red, Blue and Yellow*, a variation constructed with online application, Mondrimat. Courtesy of Dean Bruton.

Plate 2 Arc generative design using an online application by Jared Tarbell for the generation of digital designs. Courtesy of Dean Bruton and Jared Tarbell.

Plate 3 Orbital, generative design sequence.
Courtesy of Dean Bruton and Jared Tarbell.

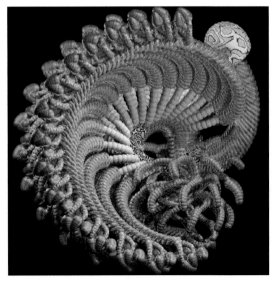

Plate 4 BRAXT. William Latham's biomemetic forms
illustrate the complexity possible in generative systems.
Courtesy of William Latham.

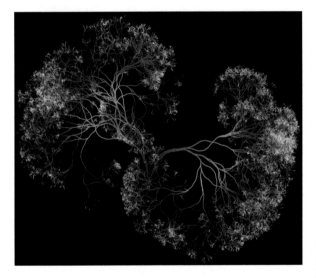

Plate 5 *Tree*, ContextFree, a downloadable program that generates images from a written grammar. The program follows the instructions to create images that contain millions of shapes. Courtesy of Xiong Lu.

Plate 6 SAr JF Skin Diagram. The Jellyfish House is a project from IwamotoScott to combine digital design, digital production and digital operation. It explores the use of emerging material and digital technologies in a house that would, like the sea creature, coexist with its environment as a networked set of distributed senses and responses. Courtesy Lisa Iwamoto; see http://www.iwamotoscott.com.

Plate 7 *Chronograph* by Tal Rosner and C.E.B. Reas (2011), a dynamic digital mural projected on the wall of the New World Centre, Miami, USA, designed by Gehry Associates and opened in 2011. Photo by Claudia Uribe. Courtesy of Casey Reas, Claudia Uribe and New World Symphony, America's Orchestral Academy.

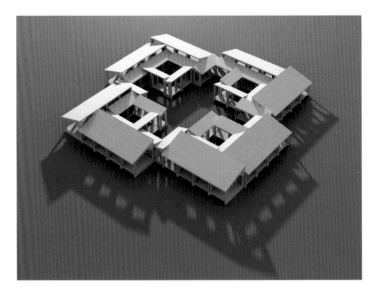

Plate 8 Bending the Espansiva house rules: a courtyard design with overlapping blocks. Courtesy of Xiong Lu.

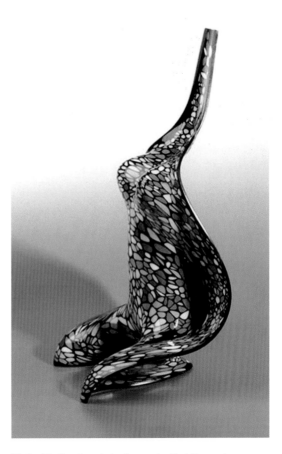

Plate 9 *Prairie House*, Chicago, Illinois, 2010. House for a fashion pattern maker and fibre artist. The skin of the building is designed to change shape in response to climate to reduce energy use. Courtesy of Tristan d'Estrée Sterk.

Plate 10 *Beast*, a chaise longue by Neri Oxman in collaboration with Craig Carter, Museum of Science, Boston, 2010. As a chaise longue, the surface contingently responds to the human body. Stood upright, the same form takes on meaning as a long-necked beast.

(a)

(b)

Plate 11 Character design inspired by the well-known Japanese Jomon ceramic sculpture style and applied to the design of a computer game proposal (a) and to a character in action (b) for the game *Tillian Tribes*. Courtesy of James Pearse.

Plate 12 The character Raphael's facial grammar displays the rules for emotional expression for the short computer animated movie *Raphael*. Courtesy of Tom Oates and Tom Lindley Donaldson.

Plate 13 Animation set construction. Courtesy of Jacob White.

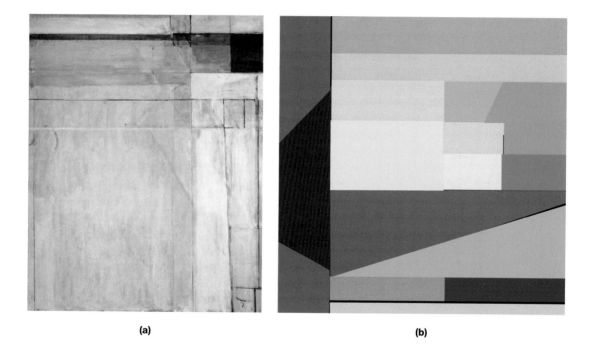

(a)   (b)

Plate 14 *Ocean Park No. 52* (a), courtesy of Diebenkorn Foundation; *Ocean Variation* (b), courtesy of Dean Bruton. Original experiment and a sampled colour variation using the Kirsch grammar for Richard Diebenkorn's Ocean Park series.

Plate 15 Reality Theatre: London Underground Evacuation Training Solution. An interactive visualization of a scenario to support situational response training using Sydac's Reality Theatre capability, demonstrating an incident and associated behaviours to determine the correct and incorrect procedures. Courtesy of Sydac Pty Ltd.

Plate 16 Using programming of digital software for commercial shoe design. Courtesy of John Maeda.

Plate 17 Design on a tartan grid exploring translucency and cut-out planes. Courtesy of Nicky Boag.

Plate 18 Studio, hard copy. The printed version contains a sample of the more extensive digital folio. Courtesy of Dahjanajay Dogra.

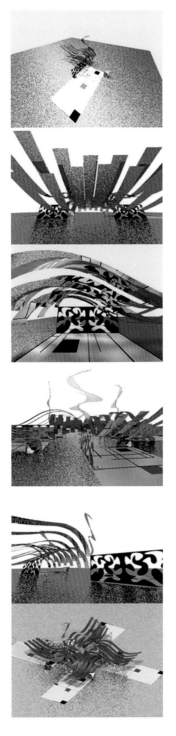

Plate 19 Stills from an animation showing movement around and through a virtual place sculpture. In the bottom images, the composition is repeated to make a more complex arrangement. Courtesy of Nikki Boag.

Plate 20 Stelton Cylinda-Line tableware designed by Arne Jacobsen in the 1960s and adapted by Paul Smith in the 2000s for a limited edition Add Colour range. Courtesy of Stelton.

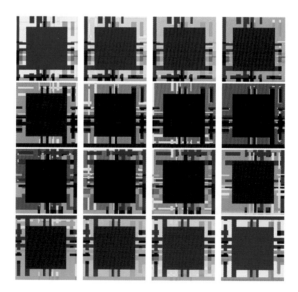

Plate 21 *Experiments in Serial Art, 1962–2010*. The composition is based on mathematical relationships between colours and forms. Courtesy of Lionel March.

Plate 22 Digital prototype showing the construction derivation of the left-hand house, beginning with concrete slab and cellar and adding in turn steel frame, timber floor joists, timber external and internal wall framing, brick spine wall (separating the two houses) and external cladding.

Plate 23 A view from the street shows how the vocabulary and rules of the traditional cottage on the right are adapted to work with contemporary ambitions for a carport, bicycle shed and bigger windows. The pattern of the neighbour's front fence is adopted unchanged for the new house.

Plate 24 *Workday Weekenders*, poster. Courtesy of Antony Radford.

Plate 25 *Take No More*, music video commission for the rock band Shiny Brights and doodles (top right), a compressed animation background computer-drawn sequence. Courtesy of Dean Bruton.

Plate 26 *CoastCity* series, 2003, the original start state and derivation #9. The colours in the derivation are samples from the original photograph. Courtesy of Dean Bruton.

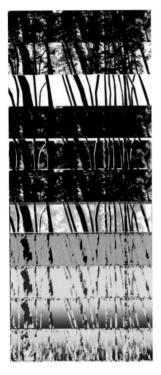

Plate 27 Bushfire regrowth, sequential development according to the contingent application of selective predefined rules. Courtesy of Dean Bruton.

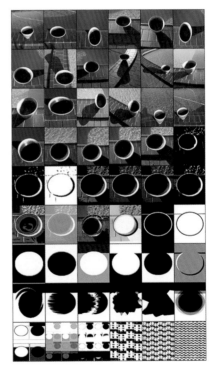

Plate 28 Bowl Series. Courtesy of Dean Bruton.

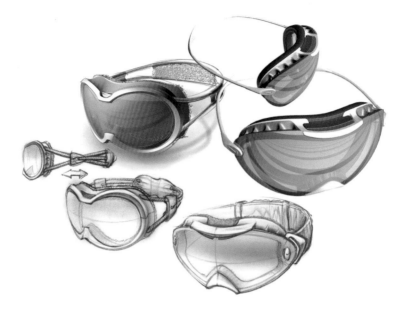

Plate 29 Design sketches and digital models of a series of goggles, with variations in patterns for both eye protection and headbands within a consistent design language. Courtesy of Gray Holland, Alchemylabs.

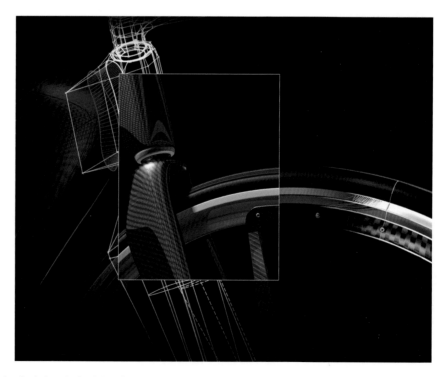

Plate 30 Design for fork and wheel rim of a bicycle, showing models in wireframe, fully rendered surface and composite forms. Courtesy of Gray Holland, Alchemylabs.

In the following sections we provide some examples of analyses, beginning with product design: a simple and elegant case of a language of tableware designed to go together in the 1960s, and the high-tech world of the Apple iPod of the 2000s.

industrial design: Arne Jacobsen's Cylinda-Line tableware

Arne Jacobsen (1902–71) was a Danish architect who also designed tableware, lights, taps and furniture.[2] He worked in the functionalist tradition, influenced by the Bauhaus in Germany and De Stijl in the Netherlands but modified by the Danish tradition of craftsmanship and expression of materials. Jacobsen was 'interested in entities—creating contexts and order right down to the smallest detail—whether he was working with architecture, furniture or applied art' (Stelton 2002: 4). The first sketches of Cylinda-Line were made in 1964, and the range was first manufactured by A/S Stelton in 1967. It immediately won the Danish Design Council's

Industrial Design Award, followed in 1968 by the American Institute of Interior Designers' International Design Award. It is represented in many design collections, including those of the Museum of Modern Art in New York and the Victoria and Albert Museum in London.

It is actually extraordinary that Cylinda-Line even exists. If today's parameters for product development, design and marketing had been followed Arne Jacobsen's rough sketches on a napkin would never have become the lovely range of stainless steel applied art which would celebrate its 25th anniversary in 1992 and is still being produced. First of all there was no technology at the beginning of the 1960s that was able to transform Arne Jacobsen's ideas about hollowware with a cylindrical overall form into stainless steel. Secondly, it was daring to launch a range of no less than 18 pieces without preliminary market research on a largely uncharted audience. (Stelton 2002)

The basic vocabulary of the language is a stainless steel hollow cylinder, circular stainless

Figure 5.2 Cylinda-Line tableware, 1967–2010, designed by Arne Jacobsen with later additions to the range. Courtesy of Stelton.

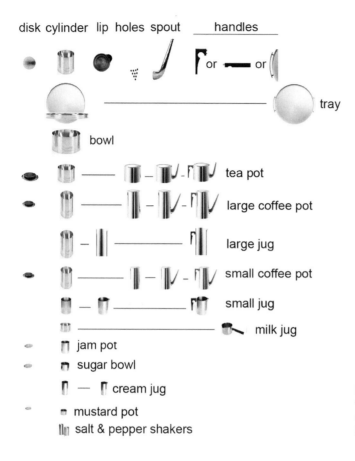

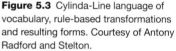

Figure 5.3 Cylinda-Line language of vocabulary, rule-based transformations and resulting forms. Courtesy of Antony Radford and Stelton.

steel disc, stainless steel spout and black nylon handle. The basic rule is that new vocabulary elements are made by minimal adaptation of existing vocabulary elements. Often, this is simply scaling in one or two dimensions of the original: a mustard pot is a small version of a sugar bowl re-scaled in height and width, while a jam pot is a larger version of the sugar bowl re-scaled only in height. The same lid fits both jam jar and sugar bowl. Other elements are segments or assemblies of this vocabulary. The handles of the tray, for example, are adapted from the surface of a cylinder, while the lid of a tea or coffee pot is made up of a large (cover) and a small (handle)

disc separated by a very thin cylinder. The nylon handle is physically and visually kept apart from the stainless steel body of a vessel by two small spacer cylinders, articulating the separation of vocabulary elements. The handles of large and small water jugs, coffee pots and tea pot are all scaled versions of the same handle form, but a low pouring jug does not have the height needed for even a scaled version of this handle to fit: it would have been too small for a grasping hand.

The solution is a wonderfully clear example of the effect of contingency on the following of rules. Rather than redesign the standard handle for all the jugs, for this one situation the typical nylon

handle is turned to be horizontal instead of vertical, and the geometry is simplified to leave only
a cut-out arc instead of the three-quarter circle.
A finger lodges comfortably in this arc. There is
a nice contrast in this difference. Indeed, one design strategy is to set up a highly ordered vocabulary and rule set, and then to selectively distort the
vocabulary and break the rule.

Over the years the Cylinda-Line range has
expanded, introducing new products. While he
lived, Jacobsen adapted the vocabulary and rules
to meet the contingencies of their individual functions. After his death, other designers continued
working with the same rules and vocabulary, following the same principle of minimal changes to
both in order to meet the contingencies of new
functions. By 2002 the range had grown to thirty-
five products, demonstrating the ability of the
grammar to encompass (with some additional
rules and an expanded but still economical vocabulary) a broadened scope.

For its fiftieth anniversary Stelton invited a
prominent contemporary designer, Paul Smith,
to design a limited edition of the range. Smith
changed just one rule at a time, keeping everything else the same.

In one set of variations, the AddColour range,
he changed the rule that the handle element is always black. Instead, the handle became available
in three colour ranges (pastel, bright and muted),
lending a playful, optimistic look to the conserva-
tive order of Jacobsen's classics. In a second set
of variations, the Statement range, the brushed
stainless steel cylindrical bodies become black
and engraved with cryptic freehand thoughts
such as 'Start something new.'

Smith probably used digital models and hence
digital design when experimenting with the introduction of colour. Indeed, the rules for generating

Figure 5.4 Cylinda-Line variations: digital models of
products (coffee pot and tea pot) and some additions that
bend the rules. Courtesy of Xiong Lu.

Cylinda-Line products can be represented digitally. If we do that, we can generate different items in the range by selecting rules and using parametric modelling with appropriate dimensions.

We can have fun, too, by generating items that bend the rules: correct in the topology of the vocabulary elements and the ways that they fit together, but incorrect in the dimensions used in the designs. We get some sculptural but often not very practical outcomes.

product design: Apple's iPod

Who designed the Apple iPod? Apple did, but they used hardware and software components from several manufacturers. For the iPod, there would almost certainly have been digital explorations of the interface, many digital tests of the components working together and the operation of the device and digital modelling of the case design leading to rapid prototyping of physical objects in resins from the digital models.

The first model was launched in 2001 (Lloyd 2004). It was designed outside-in, in the sense that Apple had a clear concept of what the product should be and the design had to match that concept (Schulze and Gratz 2011; an example of the fore-understanding described in Chapter 2). Moreover, this concept spanned technical performance, interface, the look of the product and its packaging, its presentation in Apple shops and on Web sites and its marketing. All these support and reinforce each other, with the look, feel and imagery utterly consistent.

Apple's CEO, Steve Jobs, was the driver of this vision, while Jonathan Ive was head of the industrial design team responsible for most of Apple's hardware products. The design rules and patterns of Ive's work for Apple follow principles adopted by Dieter Rams in his designs for 1960 Braun products in Germany, still seen as classics in industrial design with lasting appeal (Diaz 2008, an example of the importance of precedents).

Given this outside-in approach, on the hardware side the first task was to find a way to pack components together in as small a volume as possible: battery, hard drive, circuit board, all layered.

So the first rule of the iPod design is smallness. It is a rule that later versions of the iPod consistently follow, each one smaller and slenderer than earlier versions unless function (particularly screen size for bigger images) dictates otherwise.

The second rule is to keep the controls highly ordered and simple. In the first iPod, the face of the device had a rectangular screen with, below the screen, four buttons shaped and arranged as segments of a circle around a rotating wheel. Rotating the wheel and pushing buttons was all that was needed.

The format is strikingly similar to Rams's design for the Braun T3 pocket radio, where the rotating wheel tunes the radio under a square speaker, but any minimalist combination of rectangle and circle would tend to look like this.

In later versions, the rule of simplicity was followed by replacing the complexity and fragility of physical buttons and rotating wheel by a single touch-sensitive circle that can be both scrolled and clicked, the iPod line's signature click wheel.

In terms of the design vocabulary of the physical device, then, we have a thin rectangular box, a rectangular screen and a circular click wheel. In later iPods the screen becomes larger in comparison to the size of the device as a whole for clarity and better handling of pictures. This is all that is allowed on the face of the iPod, and even this could be reduced. In one version, the iPod

Figure 5.5 iPod Shuffle, Nano and Touch variations in style. Courtesy of Frederik Lieberath and Apple.

Shuffle, the screen is omitted altogether. In others, an updated iPod Nano and the iPod Touch, the wheel is omitted, its function replaced by button controls on the screen to be tapped, swiped, dragged or rotated, taking a pattern of user interface developed and proved in Apple's iPad and iPhone.

Other components—a Hold switch, headphone port, and a port for a connection cable to a computer—are located on the thin top or bottom edges of the case. If we lined up all the versions of the iPod from earliest to most recent, we could see how the current model has derived from earlier versions. Interestingly, the iPod Touch at the end of this sequence (in late 2010) owes its form more to the pattern and rules of Apple's iPhone than the iPod tradition. Readers will know what versions of the iPod have followed after 2010.

Steve Jobs was once a student at Stanford University. When he decided to drop out (due to a combination of cost and a sense that what he was studying was irrelevant to whatever his future might be), he went to classes on calligraphy at Reed College because he was impressed by the calligraphy he saw around the campus.

Ten years later, when he and Apple cofounder Steve Wozniak were developing the first Macintosh computer, they wondered what could make their product better than others on the market. Jobs thought of calligraphy (Jobs 2005), taking the creative step of seeing a pattern in one field and applying it in another field. Instead of the blocky green symbols on a black screen that was the then accepted standard for computers, theirs would allow real fonts, would indeed allow users to choose fonts. It was an early example of WYSIWYG (what you see is what you get), a new phenomenon in which the computer screen showed what a printed document would look like. It was also the beginning of Apple's attention to graphic design and clarity in its screen images.

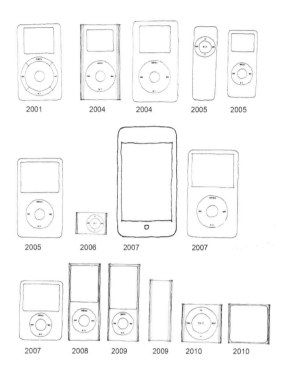

Figure 5.6 Sketches of variations in iPod designs from 2001 to 2010, from early scroll and click wheel designs to versions with no wheel, no screen and neither wheel nor screen. Courtesy of Antony Radford.

This concern for typography is evident in the small world of the iPod screen. Between 2001 and 2010 four fonts were used, starting with Chicago and ending with Helvetica. Sans-serif fonts like these have a clean, simple appearance. The look and feel of the physical device is matched in the look of the screen.

More subtly, the rule of simplicity carries through to the way an iPod operates. There are limited options, because options add complexity. In a way, the rule of simplicity also carries through to the way the company operates, producing a limited product line and succeeding by a combination of seeing product potential ('taking the best ideas bubbling up around the tech world' [Manjoo 2010: 32]), attention to detail and a sense of style.

While rigorously following its own rules, Apple succeeds by 'discipline, focus, long-term thinking and a willingness to flout the rules that govern everyone else's business' (Manjoo 2010: 26). The kinds of characteristics that we have associated with creative individuals apply equally to creative organizations.

As with the Cylinda-Line vocabulary and rules, we can play with the iPod language and generate similar-looking forms. Some of these resemble the products of other firms that have sought to emulate Apple's success. They tend to lack the clarity and discipline of the original products.

painting: Richard Diebenkorn's Ocean Park series

Richard Diebenkorn (1922–93) was born in Portland, Oregon, USA. Diebenkorn's work represents a dialogue between the influences of modernism and abstract expressionism. His life's work moved from abstraction to figurative painting and back to abstraction again. The Ocean Park series of paintings, so named for the area of Santa Monica, California, that was his final residence, feature formal, geometric arrangements of soft, often misty pastel colours. These carefully worked canvases, though absolutely abstract, emit both a glow and a sense of motion, of hidden energy. They echo his earlier, also acclaimed works: the impressions of Berkeley neighbourhoods and the expressionistic women, more formal than figurative, created in San Francisco during the 1950s and 1960s.

The Ocean Park paintings were made between 1967 and 1980.[3] Artist Robert Motherwell commented, 'There is finally a fierce beauty in Diebenkorn's work that marks a limit in our critical competence to explain it' (qtd in Danto 1997: 196).

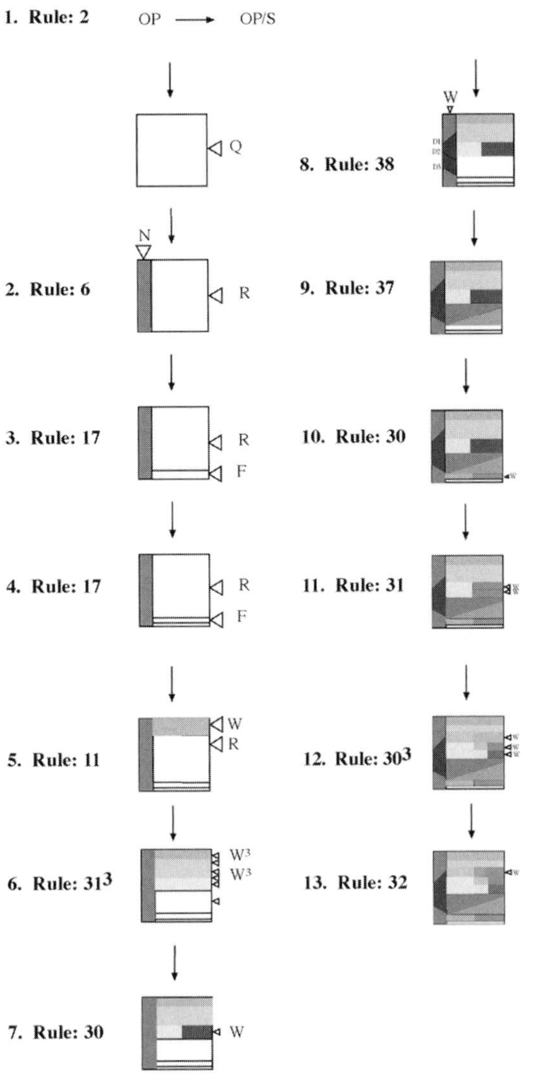

1. **Rule: 2**   OP ⟶ OP/S

2. **Rule: 6**

3. **Rule: 17**

4. **Rule: 17**

5. **Rule: 11**

6. **Rule: 31³**

7. **Rule: 30**

8. **Rule: 38**

9. **Rule: 37**

10. **Rule: 30**

11. **Rule: 31**

12. **Rule: 30³**

13. **Rule: 32**

Figure 5.7 Using the Kirsch grammar to construct a composition, then applying colours from a Diebenkorn painting in the Ocean Park series. Courtesy of Dean Bruton.

Their grammar may be defined loosely by enigmatic rules that seem to react to earlier developments in art history, including Cubism, German expressionism and American abstract expressionism (Buck 1980: 48). The influence of the work of Matisse and Mondrian is especially important. Their chief characteristics are an abstract structuring and painterly worked surfaces. Masses are represented by flat shapes with an overriding existential but holistic formal concern.

Diebenkorn spoke of rules in relation to his 1951 University of New Mexico master's project and in 1980 acknowledged his debt to modern masters. He said of these works, 'There is little of conventional fine handling or seductive surfaces in these works. They have a toughness as of the New Mexico desert. They are "right" but at the same time foreign and obviously subject only to their own rules' (qtd in Buck 1980: 55).

In 1986 Joan and Russell Kirsch showed how a syntactic description of an art work can be made with a formal grammar (Kirsch and Kirsch 1986, 1988). In a later interview, Joan Kirsch described why Diebenkorn's work was chosen for this seminal study of artists and grammars:

The proximal answer is that we had a Diebenkorn reproduction on my icebox! But, of course, it was on my ice box because I have

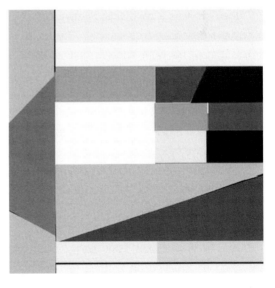

Figure 5.8 A Diebenkorn-like composition constructed with the Kirsch grammar rules. Courtesy of Dean Bruton.

Figure 5.9 *Ocean Park series No. 54*, Richard Diebenkorn, 1972. Courtesy of Diebenkorn Foundation, estate of Richard Diebenkorn.

always liked his work a great deal. Richard Diebenkorn was a good artist to start with in terms of describing a composition. That is, at first glance, his work appears geometrically formal, which might imply that he works out everything ahead of time in a cerebral fashion. But Diebenkorn said (as do most artists) 'I don't have a plan. I don't have rules.' Yet, insofar as we can recognise his work so easily, he does have rules. And so this was the challenge—to uncover his unspoken rules. (Kirsch and Kirsch 1996)

Rules for the Ocean Park series might be described as creating an alliance (or striking a balance) between structure and spatial illusion. Space is negotiated by definition and redefinition

of line and tonal fields. Lines and bars may be interpreted as spatially ambiguous. Figure-ground relationships are subdued by an emphasis on surface texture and subtle tone and colour variation. Colour is used to diminish or strengthen the key linear elements, providing a total structural and spatial unity.

The vertical format relates to views from windows, as shown in the artist's original sketches of the Ocean Park area. Flatness in the depiction of space locates the images at a relatively fixed distance from the viewer. Spatial illusions rely on the luminosity of transparent layers in some sections. Lines and shapes bleed into underlying colours or forms showing traces of previous layers of space.

The individual members of the series differ in arrangement of structure, intensity of colour and predominance of hue. Throughout the series, a familiar holistic spatial quality and sensitive surface texture is clearly recognizable. A sense of restraint is evident within the carefully placed layers of transparent veils of colour. The texture of all the works is consistently thin with some built up surfaces from successive layering. Key rules for the composition seem to be based on the speed and direction of movement of the eye around the surface of the image. For example, variations can be partly explained by differing horizontal and vertical line emphases, diagonal emphasis, edge emphasis, high key colour contrast or combinations of these.

After studying the Ocean Park paintings chiefly from reproductions, Joan Kirsch started to put together a set of rules noting which elements always appear in a painting and even the presumed order of the compositional elements. The colour and textural qualities of Diebenkorn's work posed difficult problems, but their attitude was one of let's see what can be captured rather than we can capture the essence of the entire oeuvre.

Joan Kirsch wrote a set of rules and Russell Kirsch programmed them and linked them as a formal system. The grammar consists of thirty-three rewrite rules, depicted in simple linear fashion, which may be used to derive compositional structures that emulate the paintings. A rewrite rule is one where if the pattern in the left-hand side of the rule can be matched in the image, then it can be replaced by the pattern in the right-hand side. We saw such rules in the Mondrian grammar in Chapter 1.

When Joan and Russell Kirsch generated some Diebenkorn-like compositions with their grammar they 'sent them to Diebenkorn and then phoned him expecting him to say, "Fellers, you just don't understand all the process," but he said just the opposite. His exact words were "I had the shock of recognition. Those were my compositions"' (Kirsch and Kirsch 1996).

A grammatical perspective on this work throws light on themes, concerns and decisions. It adds another dimension to previous appreciations of the work, facilitating discussion of its construction and meaning. A grammatical view enriches both art criticism and art production, and challenges those who declare they have no rule set and assume that knowledge of design behaviour is mysterious, indescribable and always incomplete.

design: Lionel March's algorithmic research

Lionel March (1934–) was influential in establishing theoretical research foundations at the Martin Centre in Cambridge during the 1970s (where he

Figure 5.10 Cover of the magazine that reported the scientific prediction of an art work's composition by Russell and Joan Kirsch, 1987.

edited *The Architecture of Form* [1976]) and later at the University of California–Los Angeles. His visual art work was influenced by serialist music and De Stijl design:

Mondrian could put a stripe down on a canvas and somehow seemed to make it important. I found that fascinating. I started arguing that it was like a composer striking one note. What happens if you strike more notes, more stripes, and what happens if you intersect these? You start playing with symmetries . . . a lot of my work was done with a musical analogy. (March 1996)

Figure 5.11 *Experiments in Serial Art*, 1966–2010.
Courtesy of Lionel March.

The 1920s German Bauhaus ideals of Laslo Moholy-Nagy and Max Bill were influential for March in his early years. Formalism has been decried by many of those who witnessed the American reductionism at work in the 1960s through the 1970s, and the 1990s showed little of interest in formalist art except in digital technologies and global communications. In this light, March's ambitions seem heroic.

> Music is kind of like a line, it's one thing to have symmetry along a line and transformations around the line but in painting you have got a two dimensional field in which you work and of course in architecture you have a three dimensional field so that the symmetries, the transformations gradually become richer and richer as you move through these dimensions, but that was the whole point of it: if musicians can do so many wonderful things around a line, effectively the time line, the duration and so on, surely we could do it. Show me an abstract work of art that has the power of a Beethoven. Why can't it have the power of a work by Beethoven? It's got more dimensions. You can do as much in two dimensions as you can do in one dimension and I don't find works that powerful. One can stand

before Jackson Pollock and it is powerful and wonderful and you kind of get absorbed in it but it just doesn't do what Beethoven seems to be able to do, or most, many musicians are able to do. (1996)

March refers to his art work as algorithmic research.

> I have for more than 30 years now, made use of rule systems in art work—things like the grids and all the rest of it that I've used consistently over a long period of time. (1996)

His response to contingency is evident in the sense of game playing inherent in his work.

> I start from some aesthetic experience which in my world I do through various games that I play with some rules that I set up a long time ago and which have been transformed since. But I know what I am doing, and as I try and develop that, I ask questions which take me back into, if you like, a reflective mode. (March 1996)

The use of rules for the artwork was inspired by an interest in both philosophy and music. March explains the basis of his approach:

It is Wittgenstein's arguments about rules: If you want to play a game you need some rules. You can play according to the rules. You can become an expert using the rules. People begin to appreciate just what you are doing and get enjoyment out of that watching the game being played. At some point or other you can, as it were, break the rules which basically means instituting a new rule which basically means introducing something else. If you play, as it were break a rule, you are going to introduce something else to take its place. I've always felt very strongly that you can clearly use it reflectively in terms of an analysis of works and so on, but you can also certainly do it the other way around constructively. (1996)

March was also inspired by artists that appeared to use rules such as Paul Klee, Wassily Kandinsky, Piet Mondrian, Mark Rothko, Richard Lose and Max Bill.

The derivations of March's art followed the musical systems set by Schoenberg, Stockhausen and Boulez, who were interested in serialism. March explains:

I was a mathematician and I was then doing architecture and I became really intrigued by the methodology which these musicians [the second Viennese School] were using to produce these aesthetic products and these expressive products. It seemed to me that the visual artist ought to be able to do very similar things, and why not. There was a play on symmetry on different kinds of scaling techniques they were using and overlays of different scales to produce new patterns, all kinds of things which were very understandable to me as a mathematician which were easily translated into graphical or visual material, pictorial material. (1996)

The designs were generated by recursive rules. By layering grids and transforming their orientation and size mathematically, March achieved many derivations with relatively few rules. The early outcome was a series of works that were composed of plastic layers of grids. These instigated paintings and three-dimensional constructions that formally used the same grammar. In contrast to the prevailing abstract expressionists' intuitive approach, March set out to use algorithmic means to define structure for his expressive purposes.

I made up some very large works using plastic and plastic film on plastic sheets, actually, so I wanted a kind of industrial approach, I wanted a hands-off from a point of view of the sort of 'touchy-feely'. I wanted to deny myself that opportunity so that if there was anything expressive in this, it was coming out of the structures that I was using and not out of the surface, not out of materiality, all the things that painters can use. I denied myself that, and these were quite striking images anyway. (1996)

March's grammatical view of his work highlights rule selection, combination and representation. His algorithmic approach denies neither an emotional expression nor a physical involvement with media.

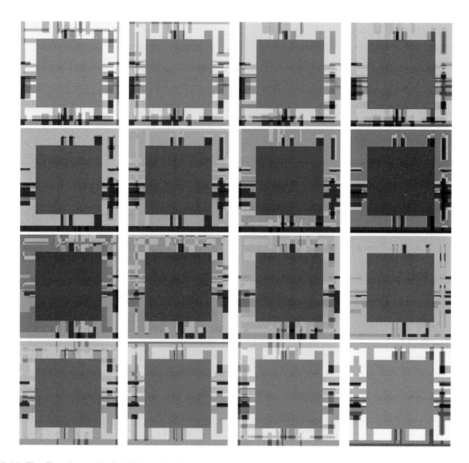

Figure 5.12 The *Experiments in Serial Art* took place at the ICA
in 1962 and was completed in 2010 in *Revolutions around Red
Square: Dusk to Dawn.* Courtesy of Lionel March.

visual simulation: Alvy Ray Smith's procedural graphics

Considered a pioneer in 3D computer graphics, Alvy Ray Smith (1943–) cofounded Pixar, the producers of the pioneering fully animated 3D feature film *Toy Story.* He contingently uses a formal rule-based grammar for some of his work. He wrote, 'My work on computer-generated plants, however, is language based, using what I call "interpretations" of formal grammar types known as L-systems, or Lindenmayer systems' (Smith 1996).[4]

Smith distinguishes between the strict formal grammar and the art in the result, which he understood as strictly his own. He explains,

The grammar emits a formal string, but it is my interpretation of that string (of 0s, 1s, [s and]s) that transforms the boring string into an interesting 'plant' (nothing like them really exists). I select the colours, the widths, the curvatures, the directions, the lighting, the 'flowering', the viewing angle, etc. There is nothing grammar-driven about these choices. Another way to say this is that there are an infinity of interpretations of a graftal grammar string. It is the artist's job to sort through these and prune the infinity down to size. (1996)

Work on cellular automata has been used for the generation of artworks based on sound (Miranda and Wanderley 2006) as well as visual elements. Smith sees the artistic process as included in the choice of sets of rules. Smith described the derivation of his work *white.sands* as follows:

This was generated using several generations of a grammar, starting with a single 'axiom', namely a single 1. The grammar has eight rules and is context sensitive. So a single 'cell' or 'segment' of the final plant (my interpretation of the 0s and 1s) changes from generation to generation according to itself (whether 0 or 1) and to its two nearest neighbour segments (whether they are 0 or 1). Some of these transformation rules do nothing. Others cause a branch to form (indicated by a [,] pair). Others cause a state change (0 to 1, for example). Others cause a splitting of a cell or segment into two—i.e. 'growth'. Note that segments, branching, growing are all parts of the interpretation of the otherwise meaningless 4-ary string generated by the grammar. So each generation is one step in a logical series of plants = snapshots of its growth. A derivation is application of the transformation rules to every cell/segment in the current generation, simultaneously, to create the succeeding generation. The artistic process includes choosing

interesting sets of rules from all those possible, choosing the interpretation parameters listed above, and deciding which generations to actually realise as phenotypes (of the string genotypes). If the piece is an animation, this adds further choices: how to interpolate the given frames to form smooth growth, the effect of

Figure 5.13 Design construction by using computer code based on L-systems, Ray Lauzzana, 1996. Courtesy of Dean Bruton.

tropisms, the path and other camera parameters, etc. (1996)

As a mathematician, Smith understood grammar and derivation as

the rules and what they apply to and how they are applied is the grammar. It is customary to define the sequence derived from application of a grammar to be the 'language' of that grammar. One can derive English sentences from an English grammar, but the sentences are considered part of the English language rather than its grammar. The grammar of DNA is well understood. The strings created are called genes, or genetic sequences, not grammar, which is only the rules used for the derivations. (1996)

Spatial relations are determined by the context of the decisions made about the derivation. This contingent sense of grammar is discussed by Smith in relation to DNA and shape grammar.

Figure 5.14 *white.sands.* 'A tribute to the beautiful White Sands of southern New Mexico, my home state, and to my father, the botanist. The flowering plants are graftals, the grasses are particle systems, the chop is my name and part of the piece. At the time, names with all lowercase letters and with dots were very unusual. The world-wide web has made them commonplace today' (Smith 1996). Created at Lucasfilm in April, 1983. Courtesy of Alvy Ray Smith.

One of the trickiest problems in mathematics and physics is the generalisation of textual notions, such as grammar and language, to graphical or pictorial elements (in case of mathematics) and to actual physical, space-occupying elements (in case of physics and chemistry). Nature has solved this problem for DNA by having the language interpreted (cf. graftals) as proteins, in a manner still not understood completely (the folding problem). One can imagine that a grammar can be expressed directly in picture, or geometric, or even molecular form. In fact, shape grammars of a very rudimentary form are about as close to this as we have come. Beyond that, the math gets very hard very fast. Certain graph grammars have stretched the bounds, but they are in general quite difficult to use. All this is strictly speaking, of course. The art world has often spoken loosely of the grammar of, say, Mondrian, or Picasso, or whoever. (1996)

Smith's work *white.sands* appears to represent a natural plant with a shadow using traditional spatial illusions based on a single light source. The combination of image with chop (the Chinese stamp) is surprising and leads the viewer to consider a more philosophical aspect of the plant by implying a connection with the iconography of Chinese calligraphy. On the difficulties of grammatical aspects of the psychological components of art, Smith comments, 'One of my beliefs is that exploration of actual grammars, as opposed to implicit ones, is one of the great uncharted oceans of art, one that the computer has uniquely made available to us artists' (1996).

Using lessons from the work of Benoît Mandelbrot[5] and others, Smith's grammatical view of

Figure 5.15 Julia set fractal image discovered by Benoît Mandelbrot. Courtesy of Dean Bruton, Creative Commons.

his own work extends beyond conventional understanding of image making. He uses grammars such as fractals to create algorithmic illusions of photographic representations of pictorial space. His imaginative possibilities are expanded by his grammatical view of representation, using computer technology to explore cellular automata. Yet he, as the artist, interprets the formal outcome from the grammar; the results of the rules are interpreted contingently.

Digital design offers ways of reexamining and redefining any traditional design process that was dependent on physical constraints and analogue time scales. After the introduction of computers to art making by exponents such as Harold Cohen, Smith offers a path for the development of software that uses data for the construction of digital form and screen-based imagery. The work of Casey Reas develops this approach and is illustrated by his work *Chronograph* with Tal Rosner on the New World Centre, the Frank Gehry–designed orchestral academy for the New World Symphony.

This application of generated imagery conceived in an art context to design is part of the digital industry production cycle not only for screen-based installations but increasingly for product designs as seen in the tableware products of Joshua Davis. Similarly, Davis has an iPhone app called Reflect, which allows users to create their own artwork Davis-style, and then view it as if through a kaleidoscope.

As we have seen in the work of artists and designers discussed in this chapter, as a result of the digital revolution, there are new ways to explore visual relationships in product design and art.

Summary: Learning from Analysis

The work those who are recognized as both highly creative and highly productive in design and art exhibits the very strong development of consistent personal grammars—and periodic, apparently disruptive but ultimately productive changes in those grammars. If we examine collections of their work, we find consistency (the repetitive use of variations of patterns and grammars), development (the gradual evolution of new patterns and grammars) and instances of minor or sometimes radical changes in response to contingencies.

chapter 6

analysis: architecture, film and games

We continue this series of analyses with examples of architecture, film and games. All include what we might call designed environments that provide the setting for activities.

can we reveal the interplay of rules and contingency in architecture, film and game design?

Film prescribes and describes activities in a fixed narrative. Games prescribe a kind of activity and the rules by which a story can develop when the game is played. Architecture anticipates a kind of activity (our examples are houses, an art museum and a conference room) but does not design that activity. As in Chapter 5, some of our case studies predate digital design but are nevertheless exemplary precedents.

architecture: Jørn Utzon's Espansiva houses

The Danish architect Jørn Utzon (best known as the designer of Sydney's Opera House) developed a theme of 'additive architecture' in his work (2009). Although dating from the 1960s and 1970s, this theme is still relevant because the repetition of standard modules is a design strategy eminently suited to the integration of digital design and construction. The architecture is hierarchical, in that the building is made up of a limited vocabulary of component modules that are in turn made up of a limited number of industrially produced building

components. Components join each other according to consistent rules, without needing to be cut or adapted. The result is a style of building that is clearly created as assemblies from a kit of parts. Utzon wrote, 'Such a pure addition principle results in a new architectural form' comparable to 'adding more trees to a forest, more deer to a herd, more stones to a beach' (1970: 1).

For a group of Danish timber merchants, Utzon designed the Espansiva building system for one-family houses. The vocabulary of modules is small, mono pitched pavilions, each with four laminated timber corner posts and insulated walls that are not load bearing, so that pavilions can be placed side by side without partitions to make larger spaces. The three different sizes of pavilions suit corridors, bathrooms, bedrooms, kitchens and sitting rooms. The rules by which pavilions can be attached to each other follow from the practical requirements of use, structure and construction, so that at least one edge of a pavilion lines up with the edge of another pavilion, and roofs slope so that they can drain into gutters along outside walls.

There is, then, a very limited vocabulary of pavilions and a very small number of rules about how they can be linked. The designs, though, can take many forms: I, L, U or courtyard layouts, or more complex arrangements that wander over a site. Utzon showed these possibilities in abstract

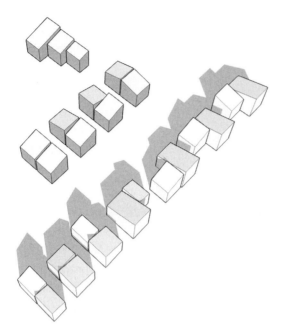

Figure 6.1 Jørn Utzon's Espansiva houses have a vocabulary of three blocks (top left) and rules about how these blocks can join together that are based on structure, construction and roof drainage. Some examples of two adjacent blocks of different sizes are also shown. Courtesy of Antony Radford.

plan drawings and with assemblies of wooden toy-like blocks.

The vocabulary and rules can be digitally modelled, replacing Utzon's wood blocks with digital equivalents. If we do that, we can explore the field of possibilities that the language of Espansiva houses makes possible. The rules we are using here are purely formal, concerned with the possible arrangement of pavilion blocks and the spaces that they enclose and divide. We could, though, add rules that concern themselves with evaluation and function. Instead of generating possibilities, we can both generate and test within the digital system. This moves us from designing with digital media to the digital system itself apparently doing the designing, albeit in a fairly simple way.

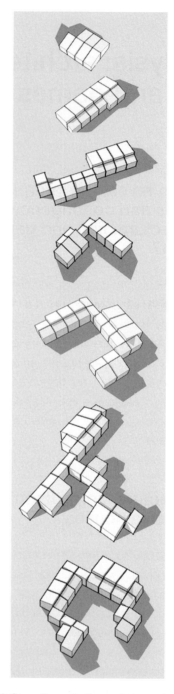

Figure 6.2 Seven Espansiva house designs using the vocabulary and rules. The top five come from designs in Jørn Utzon's book *Additive Architecture* (2009), and the sixth is Antony Radford's design using the Utzon vocabulary and rules. Courtesy of Antony Radford.

Given this simple and well-defined vocabulary and rule set, what happens if we begin to vary the rules and allow different ways for the blocks to fit together? What happens, for example, if we allow the corners of blocks to overlap? We get a style that has similarities to the Espansiva style but is clearly different. Xiong Lu, the young Chinese architect who wrote the Cylinda-Line generative system described in Chapter 5, also wrote and implemented an Espansiva generative system. The outcome is a style that is Danish-Chinese, evocative of both the contemporary order of Utzon's work and the ancient tradition of Chinese building.

In these Espansiva houses, and in Utzon's other studies in additive architecture, the components are fixed and only the assemblies vary from building to building. The components can be manufactured with numeric-controlled machinery, but there is no need for special manufacture for each building and therefore no need to take a different digital design file to the digital machine. The more demanding situation is when the components must be specially made for a project. That condition is typical of the work of the American architect Frank Gehry.

architecture: Frank Gehry's cultural icons

For most of his career Frank Gehry worked with traditional manual techniques. He began to engage in digital design simply because it provided a better—probably the only—way to represent and construct the kind of architecture that he wanted to build. Much is written already about his architecture and his use of digital media, so we look at it here only in terms of our themes in this book.

Figure 6.3 Interior of house design adapted from Espansiva rules and vocabulary, 2010. Courtesy of Xiong Lu.

Gehry started by following conventional architectural patterns—his Santa Monica Mall designed in 1980 (it has since been extensively renovated) was a commercial project that did not challenge the typology of the typical shopping mall. In his own house from the same period, though, Gehry used very unconventional patterns and an unconventional vocabulary of parts, including chain link fencing and corrugated aluminium metal sheeting. The normal rules of construction were deliberately subverted, so that the design appears as a collage of these components with, unlike in the Espansiva houses, little repetition of the way the parts connect with each other.

Gehry designed with sketches and lots of models exploring possibilities. For construction, this kind of architecture is hard to depict with conventional 2D plans and elevations, but the scale of the building was small, and Gehry was on hand to tell the builders what he wanted.

After this house, his designs became increasingly sculptural, with free-form surfaces that curve in two axes without following consistent

Figure 6.4 Frank Gehry's Guggenheim Museum, Bilbao, 1997. Courtesy of Ron Rowe.

radii. The computers were first used to describe these 3D products for construction, not to design them.

For these structures to be built, Gehry needed to fix irregular 3D surfaces in space. The CAD systems designed for architecture could not do this—they were intended for conventional architectural patterns, with few curves and even fewer that could not be defined as surfaces of spheres or other geometrically definable shapes.

One of the first of these ambitious designs was a gigantic fish-like form for Barcelona, Spain. Gehry enlisted the help of the digital media guru at the Massachusetts Institute of Technology, William Mitchell, to create a 3D digital model of this fish, but with the available software, the geometry was still not fully defined. Nevertheless, the fish was constructed. It became the starting point for a far more ambitious and hugely influential project, the Guggenheim Museum in Bilbao, Spain. Gehry designed this project with hand-drawn sketches and physical models, but he brought in Jim Glymph to help solve the problem of defining the shapes for construction.

Since software designed for architecture could not handle the task, Glymph looked to industries where the problem of defining 3D surfaces was familiar and commonplace: the aerospace and automotive industries. CATIA software was a product of the French firm Dassault. The shapes could be adjusted with a highly intuitive and predictable means of positioning the surface via control points that are located on the surface, or act as if they were connected to the surface by a rubber band. So Gehry could now have the full description of 3D geometry that he sought.

With this capability available, it would have been foolish to lose information by taking conventional 2D plans and section drawings from the 3D geometry. Instead, the model itself was used for building. On the construction site, it allowed the definition of points in space for assembling components. Off site, data from the model could be used with computer numerically controlled (CNC) machines to manufacture those components. Unlike the Espansiva houses, the components were not all the same.

> I had to come up with a method of cladding with one panel type that had to be able to change shape. That panel, shaped like an accordion, could then be predetermined in the computer. (Glymph, qtd in Van Bruggen 1997: 135)

Manufacturers provided with such information could work faster, more accurately and more cheaply. The digital model made the museum affordable.

> We found . . . that the more precise the information, the more it could be demystified and reduced to the ordering of materials of a certain shape and almost the ability of the contractor to paint by numbers. It gave the contractors security in their bid and prevented inordinate premiums. (Gehry, qtd in Van Bruggen 1997: 138)

Decisions about design form, material selection and manufacturing processes are intertwined. This does not mean that all is guaranteed to go smoothly. Contingency intervenes, necessitating adaptation and imposing its own effect on the final form.

Figure 6.5 Frank Gehry's DZ Bank building, Berlin, 1998–2000. Courtesy of Linda Theung.

Gehry's design for a conference hall in the DZ Bank, Berlin, illustrates this well (Takemori 2006; Lindsay 2001). The design took and adapted a sculptural form known colloquially as the horse's head that had emerged in the earlier unbuilt design for the Lewis house in Lyndhurst, Ohio, appropriating a pattern that had been developed for another purpose. 'All technical solutions started with the use of Gehry Partners' 3D CATIA database, but the execution development, fabrication and installation used diverse paths and varying levels of CNC [Computer Numeric Controlled] technology' (Takemori 2006: 62). The steel structure was a series of ribs, shaped to follow the inside and outside curves, defined in CATIA by a firm in Germany and CNC cut in the Czech Republic.

The interior shell of Douglass fir strips followed the internal edges of the ribs, using a mockup on one area to develop key details. The subcontractor was allowed 'enough freedom to modify the details during installation without compromising the final product' (Takemori 2006: 64).

Making the stainless steel exterior shell took several steps. From the digital model, plastic or Styrofoam (foamed polystyrene) moulds for every panel were milled by CNC routers. These were taken to the Czech Republic and used to make matching sand cast moulds, which were in turn used to make top and bottom cast iron forms for every panel. These were then transported to Sweden, where 4 mm stainless steel sheets were hot pressed to the required shapes between the forms. Because of small inaccuracies emerging during the processes of making both the press moulds and the stainless steel sheets, a second Styrofoam model was made for every panel by CNC process and used to accurately mark the edges of the stainless steel panels for final trimming.

Back in Berlin, all panels were laser surveyed into position.

> In the end, a significant amount of on-site adjustment was required to get the desired appearance because the reality was different from the computer model . . . The process produced the final desired result which was a slightly uneven, handmade quality, not a smooth finish like a car. (Takemori 2006: 67)

Although the process would differ if built today, the outcome would still be subject to the contingencies that arise in any construction process.

The experience of this and other projects led to a separate company, Gehry Technologies, and the further development of software later called Digital Project (DP/CATIA). The architecture firm, Gehry Partners, LLP, states that it 'relies on the use of Digital Project . . . to thoroughly document designs and to rationalise the bidding, fabrication and construction processes' (Gehry Partners 2010). The service offered to clients is based around the combination of Gehry's human creativity and the integration of digital design, documentation and fabrication as a way to make buildings.

film: Orson Welles's *Citizen Kane*

The 1941 film *Citizen Kane* by director Orson Welles and writer Herman Mankiewicz has frequently been critically acclaimed as the best movie of all time. It is the power and clarity of its rules and vocabulary that earn it a place in this book. Movie buffs maintain that movies reveal their genre and plot in their first three minutes. *Citizen Kane*'s opening is described this way:

> No Trespassing. The sign is the first introduction to the dark, looming, vast estate of Xanadu, empire palace of an exceedingly wealthy man. The gluttonous parade of soulless yet junk-filled space is clearly evident as we cut in towards one of Xanadu's windows; the room in which a light is shining. As we reach the window, the light vanishes, and we dissolve into a snowy blizzard. We hear the immortal 'Rosebud' mentioned; voiced by a hulking menace of a man on his last breath. The man drops dead, and the snow-scene paperweight he was holding drops to the floor and smashes. (Pour-Hashemi 2002)

Figure 6.6 *Citizen Kane* (1941). RKO Pictures, Inc. Licensed by Warner Bros. Entertainment Inc. All Rights Reserved. Note the high contrast, depth of field, low camera angle and lighting design language qualities that foreshadowed film noir.

In Chapter 3 we referred to mood, setting and format as three subgenres in film, and all are revealed in this opening. The mood in *Citizen Kane* is drama. The sign represents the barriers of the unconscious and alludes to issues of power, class and race. The meaning of the last word uttered, 'Rosebud', is the thread that we search for throughout the rest of the film. The setting is California in the then contemporary early part of the twentieth century.

The aim of the movie is to explore the life and times of Charles Foster Kane, a newspaper magnate, to understand more about the motives and machinations of the rich and powerful in society. Just as new technologies such as Facebook and Twitter reinvent the rituals of today's world, this movie explores the issues involved in establishing a new business model, in a society used to reliance on established tradition. This analysis will concentrate on the visual format of the film, attempting to discern a visual vocabulary that is linked with rules to create a new cinematic language. We begin with the vocabulary and then will consider the rules.

1. **Vocabulary.** The dominant visual elements that drive the film are qualities of the plot, themes and its use black and white cinematography. The distinctive use of the range of grays to evoke mood and space together with the strong use of dark black shadows as a character in the drama are idiosyncratic. Other vocabulary elements are captured in the application of rules such as the flashback device and the innovative use of the close-up together with a low camera angle.

2. **Themes and motifs.** Throughout *Citizen Kane*, a number of themes and motifs are explored. Some of them are the inner nature of mankind, the futility of materialism, entropy, loneliness, the impossible American dream, undependable memories, humility in old age and loss of innocence.

3. **Plot.** The plot reflects the life of William Randolph Hearst (1863–1951), who was an American newspaper magnate and leading newspaper publisher. His mansion, Hearst Castle, near San Simeon, California, on a hill overlooking the Pacific Ocean, halfway between Los Angeles and San Francisco, was the inspiration for a major part of the film's setting. The format is well known for its unique four-part story construction which uses multiple flashbacks to develop the plot sufficiently for us to understand the use of 'Rosebud' as a final death utterance.

Part of this format is the use of a film-within-a-film: the newsreel footage 'News on the March'. Audiences of the time were used to seeing the news before the screening of the main film. By inserting the newsreel at the start of the movie, the audience's comfort is dislodged because references to normality and illusion are mixed together.

4. **Rules for cinematography.** The rules for the construction of the film set a new standard for film directors to follow throughout the twentieth century. Some of the rules and patterns are these:

Black and white tonal variation A wide-ranging black and white tonal scale allows Welles to use contrast and juxtaposition of tonal elements throughout the movie. The range of tonal variation is illustrated by the use of fog in some scenes and volumetric lighting effects in others.

Moon & Sky Background Middle Distance Foreground Ground AO Practical Lights **DOF & Post**

Figure 6.7 *Carnival Night*, mood in digital lighting setup design and analysis (right), modelling by Dan Konieczka. Courtesy of Claire Kearton.

Deep depth of field Throughout the movie Welles uses a deep depth of field to show both the foreground and background in focus. This vocabulary element offers a powerful multilayer visual device as the viewer is able to interact with action in the front, middle and rear of the image.

Close-up The use of the full screen close-up to confront the viewer with the immediacy and intimacy of a scene is a core vocabulary element illustrated at the beginning of the movie when the dying Charles Foster Kane whispers, 'Rosebud'.

Close-up is again featured at the final stages of the movie when the meaning of the dying magnate's final word 'Rosebud' is revealed as the name of the young Kane's snow sled. Through the flames we see the title Rosebud engraved on the burning sled. Close-up is a means of using the camera as a commentator, a storyteller that reveals and comments on the action by juxtaposition of near and far imagery. Using the close-up in conjunction with other vocabulary elements such as flashback provides a powerful device for alerting the audience to a shift in time and space.

Camera angle Extreme camera angles are used throughout *Citizen Kane*, as in the opening sequence revealing the power of Xanadu.

Visual contrast The use of strong contrasting shapes, black juxtaposed against white, is part of the visual vocabulary of *Citizen Kane*. In some sequences we are confronted by large areas of shadow that conceal the faces of the actors and generate another kind of interpretation.

Vocabulary of *Citizen Kane*

This visual vocabulary of *Citizen Kane* can be seen throughout the movie. Rules for the development of the imagery and the construction of the story guide the development of the plot and the impact of the scenery and action.

Pan The long sequences in *Citizen Kane* were unusual at the time, and Welles was famous for pushing back the boundaries of propriety in terms of using themes of sex and politics. The long pan is often used to maximize a multilayered semantic impact.

Transition Welles applied his stage lighting ideas to his filmmaking, which resulted in memorable transitions between scenes. The light would be dimmed in the first scene and slowly raised in the second. This rule was combined with the others to great effect to convey nuances of meaning, as in a breakfast scene where the combination of transitional imagery symbolically represents the failure of a relationship.

Flashback The use of flashback occurs in a scene where a young Kane is seen playing outside the window whilst his future is signed away by foster parents inside the house. Here we see the vocabulary elements of depth of focus combined with structural flashback to create a complex revelation of the fate of the young boy as he loses his innocence to the future administrator of his life.

Figure 6.8 Film environment with Welles-style modular lights as vocabulary elements. Courtesy of Claire Kearton.

Influence of a design language

The decisive vocabulary and rule set displayed in *Citizen Kane* rarely surfaces in Welles's own later work. However, many other directors such as Jean-Luc Godard and Francois Truffaut have followed and developed this visual language in whole or in part, particularly in the two decades following *Citizen Kane*'s release.

Steven Spielberg, Francis Ford Coppola and Martin Scorsese recognize the influence of this movie. In contemporary filmmaking a flashback is commonplace, and strange camera angles and lighting are particularly associated with the science fiction genre.

Citizen Kane featured a number of cinematic innovations that are still influencing films and filmmakers to this day. The many important achievements include deep focus (in almost every scene, all objects in both foreground and background are in focus), low-angle shots, nonlinear storytelling, montage, the use of miniatures and special effects, overlapping dialogue, audio transitioning to the next scene ahead of the visual elements, a musical score that would sometimes last for only a few seconds to suggest a change in tone or emotion, unusual camera angles, lack of close-ups, linking a montage sequence with related sounds, flashbacks and flash-forwards, long, uninterrupted shots and the use of shadows (later used to great effect in the film noir genre).

Filmmaker Jean-Luc Godard summed up *Citizen Kane*'s importance by saying simply, 'everyone will always owe him everything' (qtd in Cook 1996: 420).

film and game: James Cameron's *Avatar*

While *Citizen Kane* demonstrated the potential of black-and-white light-sensitive film as a medium, the epic science fiction film *Avatar* demonstrates the potential of cinematography in digital media (*3D World* 2010). Development began with writer and director James Cameron's eighty-page script in 1994; the film was finally released in 2009 for traditional 2D viewing, 3D viewing and 4D stereoscopic viewing. Stereoscopic filmmaking was touted as a breakthrough in cinematic technology. The clarity of the rules and vocabulary helped enable teamwork; at the peak, close to 900 people from forty-six countries were working in six different locations and generating 10 TB of data each day. This is only possible if the rules are known.

The film broke several box office records during its release and became the highest-grossing film of all time worldwide, surpassing Cameron's *Titanic*, which had held the records for the previous twelve years. It also became the first film to gross more than $2 billion. *Avatar* was nominated for nine Academy Awards. Following the film's success, Cameron signed with 20th Century Fox to produce two sequels, making *Avatar* the first of a trilogy.

Plot

The film is set in 2154, when humans are mining a precious mineral called unobtanium on Pandora, a lush moon of a gas giant in the Alpha Centauri star system. The expansion of the mining colony threatens the continued existence of a local tribe of Na'vi, a humanoid species indigenous to Pandora. The film's title refers to the genetically engineered Na'vi-human hybrid bodies used by a team of researchers to interact with the natives of Pandora.

Avatars are used by humans to infiltrate, gain intelligence and persuade the Na'vi community to cooperate with the miners. Wounded and wheelchair-bound human Jake Sully is trained to remotely operate an avatar. Via his avatar, Jake meets and falls in love with the Na'vi princess Neytiri, and comes to recognize that the life and values of her kind are superior to the exploitative values of the miners.

Patterns in the plot are discernible by comparison with the genre of cowboys and Indians (for example, TV shows and movies about Tonto and the Lone Ranger, plus a love interest) in the unfolding of the story line. The plot is set in a strong and impressive digitally designed visual vocabulary of Pandora that is based on a vocabulary of an Earth environment, but everything is exaggerated, so that trees are gigantic, and the lighting and mood of the natural landscape is magical.

The grammar of the Na'vi

The Na'vi have distinctive visual characteristics. This alien race is three metres tall with blue skin,

Figure 6.9 Chinese mountain landscape suggestive of the *Avatar* game environment, 2010. Courtesy of Dean Bruton.

pointed ears and tails. They have muscles, skin and tendons; think like humans; express emotions like humans; have social structures like humans. Gareth Griffiths (drawing on writings by Richard Rorty) comments that

> we can't even begin to imagine what other civilisations on other planets are like . . . or even what the environment would look like, so we will always end up representing our own, save for an extra eye here, longer ears or funny marks above the eyebrows there, and depicting the skies and earth in electric tones. (2010: 4)

In the production process, images of human actors and computer graphic models are placed side by side, and the model is adjusted to capture the nuances of expression of the human— copying the human rules and vocabulary. The Na'vi are idealized versions of humans—there seems to be no sign of an overweight Na'vi although elders are part of the tribe. The game characters emulate the film characters and have the same names, including Na'vi names such as Tan Jala, Beyda'amo and Tsahik Sanume.

The grammar of the Pandora landscape

The visual elements of the Pandora landscape are rich and lush so as to evoke a jungle landscape based on scenery such as rocks in the Huangshan mountains of China. Some of the plants are generated through procedural foliage software, some modelled by hand. Making the landscape involves the use of digital design processes such as procedural terrain, which uses fractal rules of self-similarity to shape itself. But on Pandora not all plant life is subject to the laws of gravity—as

well as plants rooted in the ground, others are magnetically suspended in space. Here we see new contra rules for landscape design.

The grammar of machines and weapons

The equipment used by the protagonists is based on the construction rules and appearance of early twenty-first-century steel machines used by the military on Earth, but the scale and complexity factor exaggerates the power and range of the weaponry and transport vehicles.

The themes

The message encompasses contemporary Earth issues of sustainability, the battle between exploitation and sustainability, the struggle between the powerful and the weak, and how in the David and Goliath tradition it is possible for the apparently weak to fight evil and win.

Avatar the game

The visual design of the *Avatar* game closely resembles the movie. The creatures, landscape and objects are consistent with the rules and patterns established in the movie. The illusion of photographic reality is somewhat muted by the need for low polygon models and game-style movements. The game's rules aim to provide an adventure in the world of Pandora. The player's task is to pilot his or her own avatar, a hybrid of the player's DNA and that of Pandora's indigenous species, the Na'vi. As the player ventures into the Pandora environment, new discoveries are made about the Na'vi, their struggle to prevent the conquest of Pandora and their allegiances to either side of the conflict.

The grammar of game play creates a new experience that embarks on an alternative reality

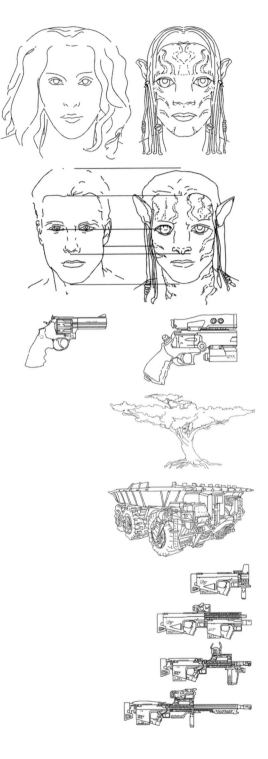

only available for the game environment. Players ride horses, fly dragon-like creatures and operate weapons, but at a pace dictated by the player. The video game world has a life of its own marked by consistent digital design patterns and offers entry through direct connection with one's own custom-designed, rule-based appearance.

Summary: Making Patterns and Grammars Apparent

In this and the previous chapter we have examined the patterns and grammars that can be seen in a variety of kinds of design. The most important point to be made from this series of analyses is that whatever the design field and mode of presentation, the basic concepts of rules and vocabulary in patterns and grammars can be found and made apparent.

Figure 6.10 Sketches of transformations of female and male faces and a handgun found on Earth (left) into modified forms that might be found on Pandora (right). Similar transformations of Earth-forms by modification, addition and exaggeration can be found in the trees and vehicles of Pandora. Variations are found, as in a language of guns. Courtesy of Dean Bruton.

chapter 7

serious play

As a means of developing our skills, we want to promote a case for play, not with interactive digital games but as players in the engrossing game of creating and making designs.

how can we develop digital skills and creativity through play?

Why work when we can play? In this chapter, we look at studio scenarios we have conducted with students of art, design, architecture and landscape architecture (Radford 2000; Bruton 2007, 2011). Here we can find explicit design projects (we shall call them games) where those engaged in the studio work have been challenged by broad game rules and game goals. These games are always open ended, with clear and attainable design objectives but offering opportunities to go beyond the expected.[1]

The essence of games lies in our immersion in play that is subject to rules. Immersion implies a complete absorption in the activity: 'in this intensity, this absorption, this power of maddening, lies the very essence, the primordial quality of play' (Huizinga 1970: 21). This absorption must be willing: 'First and foremost . . . all play is a voluntary activity. Play to order is no longer play: it could at best be a forcible imitation of it . . . Play is not "ordinary" or "real" life. It is rather a stepping out of "real" life into a temporary sphere of activity with a disposition all of its own' (Huizinga 1970: 26). Play licenses us to neglect practicalities and expectations, to take risks and to suspend our sense of what is possible.

The German philosopher Hans-Georg Gadamer has written on 'the way in which the rules of a game relate to its playing . . . The rules provide a framework for the playing of the game and determine the range of appropriate actions the players can take, but they do not account for the way the game is played or the way it turns out each time it is played' (qtd in Snodgrass 1991: 5). Indeed, the rules may change many times in the course of the play.

According to Johan Huizinga, all manifestations of civilization—religious ritual, language, law, war, science, poetry, philosophy and art—are essentially forms of play. Eric Berne, in *Games People Play* (1964) draws attention to the way people act as if they are playing games in the various circumstances of life. But a sense of play assumes relative safety, that the adverse consequences of poor play are always limited. There is the spice of danger, but never a debilitating fear of failure.

We have seen that the characteristics of digital media lend themselves to a grammatical focus.[2]

Play and Games

The presence of rules is the essential difference between play and playing games. All games have rules; even the free play of childhood is frequently subject to implied and agreed-upon rules that are interpreted by the players.

In this chapter we discuss how a set of digital games are played, with the results and the processes of playing. The games are organized into three groups:

1. **The series.** The first group emphasizes the notion of series and derivation, primarily in 2D but extending to vocabularies of 3D shapes. The aim is to make many instances of designs within a language that are all derived in similar ways with essentially the same grammar and patterns.

2. **The fabrication.** The second group emphasizes the notion of fabricating digital 3D objects and places, using defined spatial organizations or restricted vocabularies as the bases for the games. The aim is to work towards a 3D system of form making in which various elements of the piece are ordered according to predetermined rules and variations on them.

3. **The surreal.** The third group emphasizes the surreal, the boundary between the apparently real and surreal, and how variations in expected grammatical attributes and relationships lead to a sense of the surreal. The aim is to explore how bending the implicit and usually unacknowledged rules of the so-called real-world leads to the making of surreal virtual worlds.

It is how these games are played that matters. The successful studio is characterized by a vibrant creativity, the games being starting points for us to produce results outside expectations. Game On!

Figure 7.1 Computer graphics commercial for a newspaper, *Trading Post.* Courtesy of Jacob White.

the series

A series is 'a number of things of one kind . . . following one another in temporal succession, or in the order of discourse or reasoning' (*Oxford English Dictionary* 2011). The notion of series is a very common strategy in both Eastern and Western traditions of art and design. Islamic art is based on regular thematic schemas, as are Indian miniatures, Japanese printmaking and traditional Chinese architecture. Often the series emerges post facto, identifiable after creation (perhaps over many years) by commonalities in composition rather than initial intention. In the terminology of patterns and grammars, a series rarely enumerates the whole of a design language, but by presenting multiple instances, it may give a far more complete impression of the possibilities within that language than any single work can offer. For artists, using a theme for the conceptual underpinning of visual investigations provides a basis for comparison and reflection. Thematic

Figure 7.2 *Postcard*, 2009. The sequence of images (read left to right, row by row) explores the sequential effects of filters and transformations on an original photograph of the Sydney Opera House. Courtesy of Jun Cai.

devices are also a good way to begin design explorations because they force the development of options. Our grammatical series games variously emphasize commonality of rules, derivation, and interpretation.

Game 1.1

A postcard. Using the theme Traces and Layers—Searching for Self Identity, produce 54 images for a postcard that develop a single image. Keep the variations in sequential order so that the process of discovery is apparent. Develop the imagery in concept and scale after considering the strengths and recurring qualities that emerge.

The idea of this postcard game is to explore a personally significant image using software (Photoshop) that provides filters and graphics editing tools.

This simple design game demonstrates some fundamental components of a grammatical focus in a series: an initial or start state (the first image), lexicon (additional images or icons) and a set of operations (filters and graphic editing operations). It also forces selection and rejection from a much larger range of design outcomes.

Game 1.2

A personal directory of shapes. Design a set of shapes that represent each letter of an alphabet.

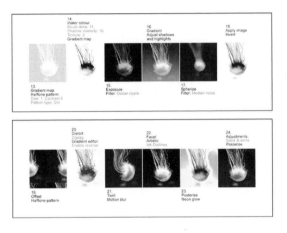

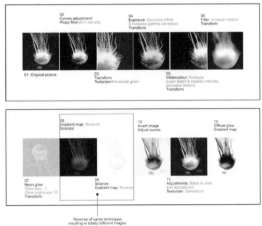

Figure 7.3 Storyboard explaining how a sequence of images in a postcard was derived by transformation of an image. Courtesy of Basyarah Hamat.

The letters should explore both symmetry and asymmetry, and use single and multiple colours in 2D (and optionally 3D) textual experiments.

Just as a graphic designer or artist might use a specific set of visual elements for the composition of a poster or painting, so, too, the choice of a set of shapes for a personal shape directory may shed light on a personal aesthetic. Once the vocabulary is designed, it can be explored in static and animated imagery using visual representations of the translations of poems and text.

the fabrication

A fabrication can simply be a construction, but it can also be 'a false statement; a forgery' (*Oxford English Dictionary* 2011). We draw on both of these meanings: the sense of making, production and craft, and also the sense of something alluding to or masquerading as something else. All these games are ambiguous about whether the intention is digital fabrication alone, with no reference to fabrication in the real world, or digital

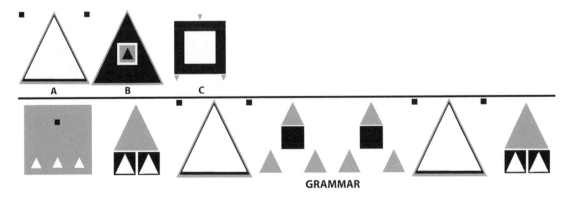

Figure 7.4 The word 'grammar' written in shape letters that replace the conventional letters of the alphabet. Courtesy of Neal Powell.

Figure 7.5 Design on a tartan grid. In this example the
panels have the materiality of physical materials. Courtesy
of Andres Torres.

fabrication as a precursor for physical realization
as architecture or urban design. For example, the
first game specifies dimensions for a grid and panels, inviting a mental populating of the fabricated
object with people and providing a sense of scale
and tangibility. Yet there are deliberate incon-
gruities; the panels are not expected to be self-
supporting or even to be spatially continuous, so
that the object in the real world would need to
rely on fabled sky hooks to be constructed. In the
second game, virtual block land, there are no dimensions, but there are labels which suggest real-
world elements. The results could almost (again,
needing a few sky hooks) be built. The hints that
these could be physical objects leads us to view

them with the expectations that we apply to physical objects, sharpening the sense of delicacy,
suspension and intensity of light and colour that is
possible because of their actual virtual existence.

Game 2.1

Designs on a tartan grid. Make a virtual sculpture
based on a nine square grid, which in body space
would be 1,200 mm × 1,200 mm (4 ft × 4 ft) with
600 mm (2 ft) separating zones between the
squares. All the panels are 2,400 mm (8 ft) high
and located on the grid. The ideas should explore
symmetry and asymmetry, single and multiple colours and designs and the effect of breaking the
grid.

The grid has a long history in design. It underlies the spatial organization of classical architecture (Tzonis and Lefaivre 1986) and much contemporary architecture. The nine square grid, and its expansion as a tartan grid, is the basis for many of the villas of the Italian Renaissance architect Andrea Palladio. This game uses the grid to provide order. It invites a concern for the surface qualities of the panels; degrees of transparency and translucency, and the overlaying of surfaces as panels are seen through other panels; the definition of space using panels as boundaries. We can imagine what it would be like to walk between these panels, and the feelings of enclosure and exposure that would result.

After the grid, the next game invites us to play with scale (would the blocks we make be large or small in body space?) and imagine urban places or interior designs.

Game 2.2

Virtual block land (additive play). Make a vocabulary of five elements, to include a platform element, a linear element, a canopy element, a wall element and a point element. These can be interpreted broadly. Use the vocabulary to make design compositions using each element exactly once. Group the composition, and use that in making more designs which keep the spatial relationships of the original composition. Annotate the images with names that suggest aspects of the physical world that they evoke.

Making things with blocks is a part of most people's growing up. A child's set of brightly coloured wooden blocks to touch, taste, throw and place is a fundamental part of the exploration and realization of space and the extent of the body. Sets of blocks take many forms: off-cuts from the carpenter's shop, with no two blocks the same

Audio Play

With a digital audio player, we can have our own sound track as we move through the physical world. In the virtual world, a fly-through casts us in the role of a film director, thinking how to best design the camera route to show the form and to create an effective ride. We might begin to think of this ride when we design the form.

size, some rectilinear, others at the strange angles of the piece left over; classic sets such as Froebel blocks, designed in Germany in the 1830s by the founder of the kindergarten, Friedrich Froebel, or Cuisenaire blocks, designed by the French educationalist Cuisenaire, or the brightly coloured wooden blocks of Enid Blyton's Noddy land or the finely engineered plastic blocks of Lego and Lego land. There are blocks of the toyshop and blocks of the art gallery: recent sets of Gothic and classical building elements available for purchase in design shops and the sale by the Frank Lloyd Wright foundation of a set of maple wood Froebel blocks costing several hundred dollars. There are also puzzle blocks, such as Piet Hein's SOMA cube of interlocking hardwood blocks in a $3 \times 3 \times 3$ cube.

As media for design and building, sets of blocks prescribe a vocabulary of elements with which to work: for example, the twenty-one one-inch cubes, six half cubes and twelve quarter cubes in the Gift 5 of the Froebel blocks. The shapes available limit the nature of what can be built, while the number of blocks in the set limits its extent. There are rules, too: the rules of gravity control the way towers can be built (horizontal plane onto horizontal plane); the keys and sockets of Lego blocks prescribe implicit rules about the form of Lego land. Blocks make patterns of shape and colour, and cause further patterns of

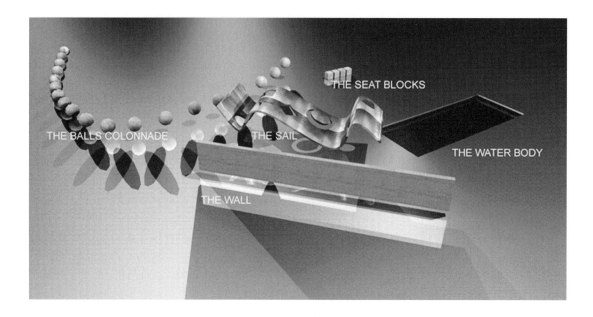

THE SEAT BLOCKS

THE BALLS COLONNADE

THE SAIL

THE WATER BODY

THE WALL

Play in a Virtual Space

Many of the attributes of the physical world can be simulated: the tactile sense, smell and the sound of the clack as virtual block is placed on virtual block. With a digital 3D stereographic vision, we can make quick head movements to look around corners to get a different view. We also open new spatial form possibilities.

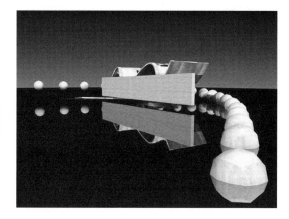

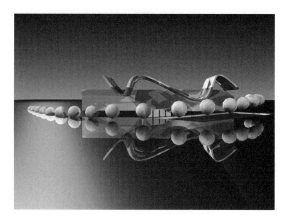

Figure 7.6 Additive play: the scene is assembled from elements that have equivalents in the physical world. Courtesy of Andres Torres.

light and shade. In playing with blocks, there are elements of abstract composition at a beginning stage, the results regarded and examined by the playing child. More often, toy people populate the blocks: wars take place; babies are tended; farms prosper. The blocks take on meaning as houses, battleships, cars, shops, cradles and spaceships; forms of life (representing real-world objects) as well as forms of knowledge (about geometry and parts–whole relationships) and forms of beauty (abstract patterns) (see Froebel 1912).

What happens when we move from a physical to a virtual world? We can shape our own blocks; we can have an infinite number of them; we can fix or free the spatial relationships; we can merge the blocks, defy gravity, change their colour; we can see views that could only be gained by flies on ceilings or worms under the floorboards in the physical world. Playing games with virtual blocks is not the same as playing games with physical blocks, but it, too, prompts flights of imagination, fun and discovery. The emphasis, as with real blocks, is both on the compositions of arrangements of the blocks (akin to Froebel's 'forms of beauty') and on their interpretation as real-world objects (akin to Froebel's 'forms of life').

Our rules are to some extent arbitrary, and games can be played with different rules. Our first rule is that there is a limit to the number of different blocks a player may have, although a single block may be made up of several disconnected elements as long as the spatial relationships between them remains constant. The second rule is that the interpretations as real-world objects should primarily come from the world of the built environment: shops, hotels, houses rather than cars, battleships and aeroplanes.

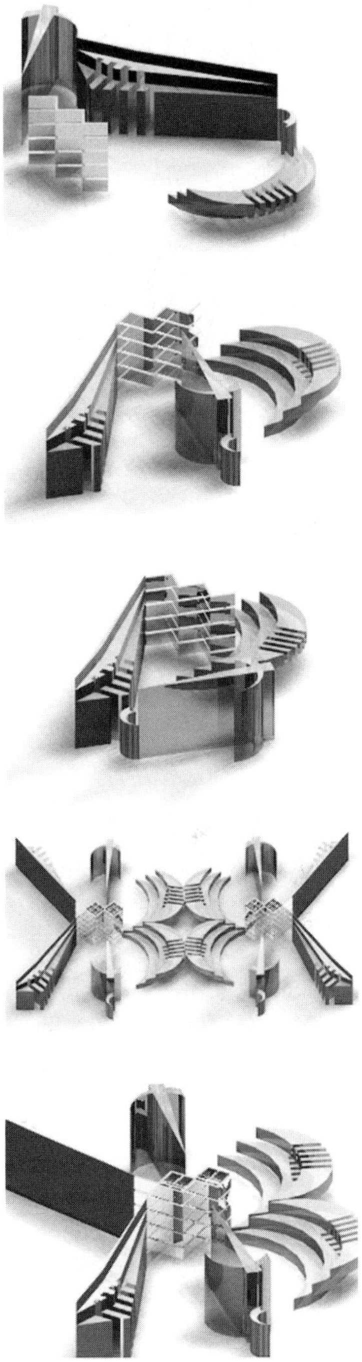

Figure 7.7 Five compositions made by assembly and repetition of a vocabulary of elements through translation, rotation and reflection. Courtesy of Nikki Boag.

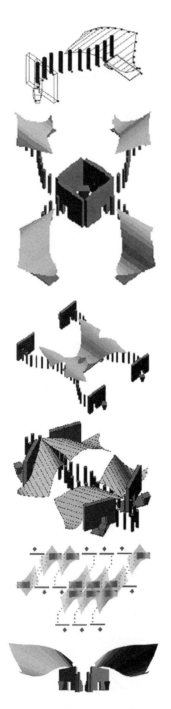

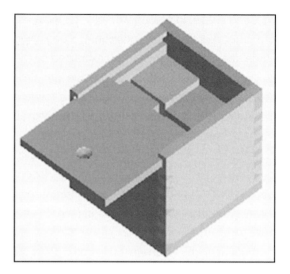

Figure 7.9 Froebel blocks kit: digital model of the physical box and small set of four blocks. Courtesy of Antony Radford.

Figure 7.10 Froebel blocks assemblage: assembling the virtual blocks without the constraints of the physical blocks. Courtesy of Antony Radford.

Figure 7.8 Designs with five elements of colonnade, door, platform, sail and block to make spaces with different characters. From top: the path, the centre, the two-way stage, the avenue, the resort and the entry. Courtesy of Peter Schumacher.

First, we make five blocks. Each element has its own interpretation, and we give them names (ideas of 'forms of life' right from the start). By combining elements, more complex readings arise. This choice is not arbitrary. Rather, it comes from a to and fro between the individual elements and experiments with their arrangement. What blocks allow for interesting configurations? What blocks allow for interesting interpretations?

As the blocks are arranged and combined, new interpretations inevitably arise. What does this composition suggest as a fragment of the built environment? Can that suggestion be clearer, richer, more evocative? With the use and re-use of chosen arrangements the possibilities of the original configuration of five blocks is of lesser importance than the possibilities of the spaces left over between their repeated instances. The scale is not lost, but the possibilities become more complex and varied.

Game 2.3

Negative virtual block land (subtractive play). Take a rectangular block. Using Boolean operations, subtract parts of the block using a vocabulary of five solids to make an interconnected series of spaces hollowed into the surface of the block.

The games above are essentially additive in nature—a vocabulary of elements is created and assembled in creative ways. Sculpture often operates differently, beginning with a block of stone or wood and chipping away to reveal the form. The mechanized processes of milling and turning operate in a similar way. These are subtractive in nature. So, too, is the process of casting, where the final artwork is the negative of the originally created form. In this game the idea is to begin with a solid—or perhaps a number of solids—and subtract volumes to create the work. The point here is to see form in a different way, as what is not there rather than what is there.

All these fabrications—the tartan grid, the virtual block land and the negative virtual block land—can be explored via fly-throughs and flybys, or by representing the fabrications in environments that can be explored interactively. Architecture, interior design, landscape architecture and urban design are all experienced more by moving through than as static scenes. In the next game, the purpose focuses on the ride.

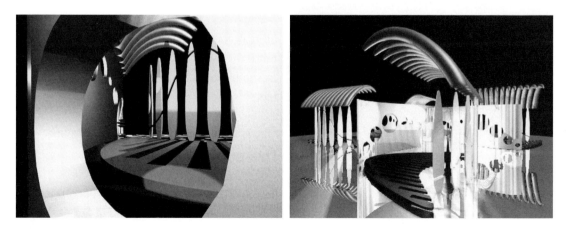

Figure 7.11 Detail and overview from a five element design. Courtesy of Carla Lepore.

Game 2.4

A grammatical luge. Design, construct and direct a short trip through a grammatically designed world, travelling at speed along a luge-like track

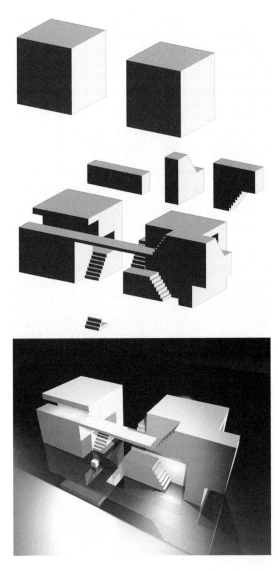

Figure 7.12 Subtractive play: an accompanying animation leads the viewer around the composition and up and down the steep steps, flying out into space to make the turns easier. Courtesy of Andres Torres.

through enclosures, over gaps, between constrictions. Add a sound track.

We are familiar with the luge from the Winter Olympics: that dangerous event where one or two people lying face up and feet first on a sled hurtle down a preformed channel in the snow. The channel is always highly grammatical, following implicit rules of colour (white) and form (curving edges that allow the sled to be steered up the side at bends) as it snakes down the hillside. Seen from a camera mounted at the front (we have no first-hand experience), signs, bridges and people flash past the speeding sled. Each descent is an aesthetic, art-like dynamic experience. The goal of this game is to replace the grammar of white snow and curving form with another grammar of colour and form, and to see the trip from that camera at the front of the notional sled. The emphasis is on movement with elements seen briefly as they are passed, without time for detail. The route can tell a story or be a purely sensuous experience.

We might set the trip to music, matching the drama of the ride with the tempo, rhythms and crescendos of sound. As with the previous games, the outcome can be interpreted as built form in body space. This might be intended, as in a ride through a city or a subway, or merely one of many interpretations of ambiguous form.

the surreal

Surrealism was a movement in art and literature, from about 1919 on, that aimed at expressing the subconscious mind through techniques including the 'irrational juxtaposition' of realistic images and

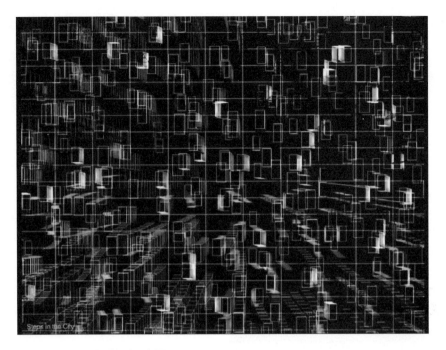

Figure 7.13 Still from *Steps in the City* (luge). The animation has an equally grammatical soundtrack. Courtesy of Verdy Kwee.

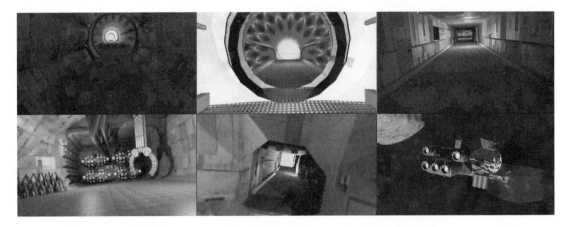

Figure 7.14 Stills from *Luge*. Courtesy of Michael Nixon.

the creation of mysterious symbols (*Oxford English Dictionary* 2011).

As soon as we make an object in the digital as well as in the physical world, we interpret it.

An object or scene appears surreal when these interpretations are at odds with our expectations of the real. Virtual space has inherently surreal qualities—designs made in virtual space can defy

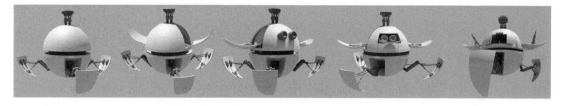

Figure 7.15 Model of a robotic security system composed of modular units. Courtesy of Michael Nixon.

real-world rules. There is no gravity and no need for supports. There is no limit to viewing positions. The scale relationships that are familiar in the real world no longer apply. In the words of one game player, it is 'a world of endless possibilities and dreams' (Boag 1999).

Figure 7.16 Analysis and change: *Cool Gerberas.* Courtesy of Carla Lepore.

Game 3

Analysis and change. Analyse an object or small group of objects in terms of vocabulary and rules. Make changes to the vocabulary or the rules so that the interpretation is unsettled.

This is a two-part game. The first part draws on reality, seeking to analyse and represent a natural or human-made object in terms of its vocabulary and rules. The analysis will be an abstraction, picking out what to represent. By making changes to vocabulary and rules in the second part, the object is shifted from reality to the unreal—escaping the control of reason. A new understanding of the image arises, one that is not so easily drawn from our experience of reality. In this game we contrast the initial straightforward

Figure 7.17 Three stills from *Imaginative Worlds* (luge). Courtesy of Tain Patterson.

task of interpretation and analysis with the following imaginative juxtaposition of playful ideas and forms.

By extending this process to encompass an environment rather than an object, we can design an imaginative world that appropriates the familiar vocabulary of the physical world but adapts it by ignoring some (but not all) of the constraints of the physical world. Like the landscapes of Salvador Dali, these places are not faithful representations of Earth places, but we can still recognize the parts and imagine how we would navigate around them.

The landscape of Pandora with its islands in the air that we found in the *Avatar* film and game is just such a surreal place. For humans, this kind of adapted landscape tends to be a much more interesting place than an entirely made-up landscape without the references to and appropriation of our Earth world.

and now for something completely different

The grammatical games that have been described in this chapter are outcomes from studios linked by their focus on form and grammar within digital design domains. They take place in a framework of reflective practice. Those who are immersed in these grammatical studios adopt techniques of journaling and annotations to record their reflections. In a group, we are also encouraged to critique each others' work, to share interpretations, to help each other in the use of software and media and to go further by suggesting possible ways to develop work. This combination of playful making and

Figure 7.18 Stills from *Three Environments* (luge). Courtesy of Tom Oates.

reflective recording, always pushing boundaries and seeking the unexpected, makes the grammatical virtual or nonvirtual studio a highly effective site for developing skills in design and creativity (Bruton 2010).

A British television series from the 1970s, *Monty Python's Flying Circus*, used the phrase 'and now for something completely different' to link unrelated comedy sketches. It is a good motto for the playful design studio. When we

Figure 7.19 Five element environment used as a luge-like track for a short movie. Courtesy of Basyarah Hamat.

get stuck, or equally when we get rather too pleased with ourselves about our work, it is a good idea to try something 'completely different'—different rules, different vocabulary and different interpretations of the game we are playing. We can always return to the point we have reached if we want to do so later. That way, the studio becomes a joyous, crazy, playground of ideas.

Summary: Recording Serious Play

Experimenting playfully with vocabularies and rules, just for the fun of it, is a great way to develop our range and competence in digital design.

Annotated logbooks—physical or digital— help in developing a habit of reflective practice. As a part of this practice, we should watch for and record the demands of contingency, the nature of the rules that are used—and how and when they are broken or recast—and the derivation of our work.

chapter 8

studio journals

In this chapter we show that when we design, we practice what we write. More than a record, these pages reveal the discourse we carry within: past voices, speculations, critiques and dreams.

what is the interplay of rules and contingency in our own designs?

What do we do—that is, Dean and Tony, the authors of this book? We engage in the reflective practices of writing, teaching, research and design—and the reflective practice of living in its broadest sense. Here, we look back to our journals and describe some of our design processes. We concentrate on the vocabularies, rules, and contingencies encountered in the process. We refer to the patterns used and look for creativity. This does not mean that we claim exemplary creativity in this work. That is not necessary; since creativity is a value perceived rather than a measurable attribute, the degree of creativity can remain a moot point.

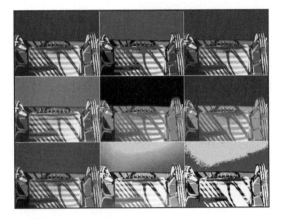

Figure 8.1 *Cane Chair Series*, exploring rules in filters, computer graphic on canvas, 1996. Courtesy of Dean Bruton.

Reflection and Dialogue

Readers may skip this chapter without missing the major points of this book, but it provides an entry into the process of self-reflective dialogue. Examples 1, 3, 5 and 6 are Dean Bruton's accounts of some of his work, whilst examples 2 and 4 are Tony Radford's accounts of some of his work.

Figure 8.2 Study for a tower building, 2011, adapting and combining patterns drawn from the architecture of Oscar Niemeyer, Jean Nouvel, Mies van der Rohe and (in the expressive service core) Louis Kahn. Courtesy of Antony Radford.

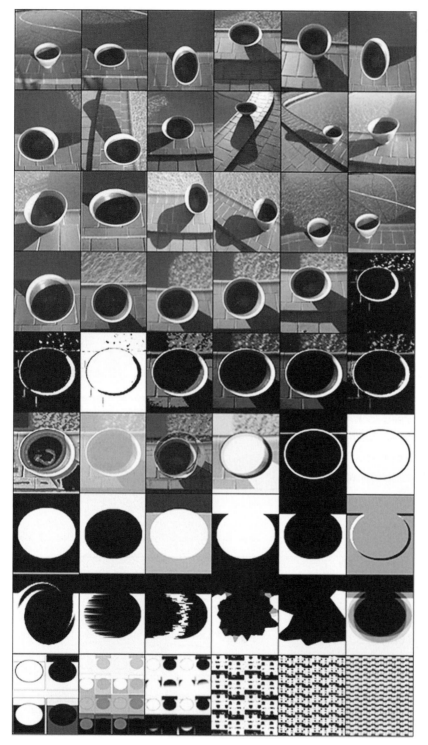

Figure 8.3 Bowl Series, 1996. Courtesy of Dean Bruton.

Figure 8.4 Bowl Series, 1996. A ceramic bowl is the starting point for a visual adventure.

Figure 8.5 Bowl Series, 1996. Chart of turning points.

example 1: the Bowl Series (Dean)

The selection of a subject for study is often difficult because the reasons for an image to signify more than a trivial meaning are elusive. Sometimes it seems that in the early stages, doing may be more productive than thinking it through. I was motivated by the then seemingly generous theme of objects. I was limited to those things close by as I left the indoor studio with camera in hand to explore the swimming pool area outside. For a key subject I chose a ceramic bowl to see if it might offer some visual delights. Made by Australian potter and friend Marianne Cole, the stoneware bowl had lived with us in the dining room for many years. It has a glaze that connects with a tradition of Australian matte glazes (and reminds me of personal links with Australian ceramicists Milton Moon, Derek Smith and Les Blakeborough). It speaks to me of the many hours of working with clay, fire and glass to evoke a special form and physical relationship between these physical substances and an inner sense of coastal landscape.

Some colours were almost complementary: turquoise and light mustard; yellow with the deeper blues of the water being a significant backdrop for the paver pinks. I took the digital images quickly with little but intuitive planning—front, back, side, and three-quarter views. Back inside the studio, I was disappointed with the images on the computer screen because the colours were weak compared to the strong Australian light of the original visual experience. I altered the colours and began to impose a system of simpler flat colour areas on top of the core shapes. This led to a variety of exciting colour combinations. I sought a system for the sequence of derivations and contemplated a return

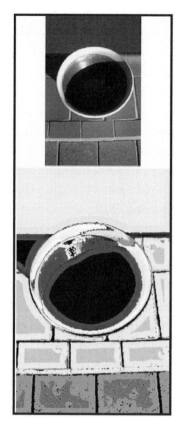

Figure 8.6 Photoshop experiment: Bowl Series,
#1copymax/blend/sens, 1996. Before the History menu
was added to the software, exploring the idea of coding the
image names to record transformations.

to rules and variations for my next visual experiments. The Bowl Series sequence reads from left to right, and top to bottom in the resulting poster. My strategy was to retain the essential character of the image while parametrically changing the formal variables.

With this intention in mind, I explored the relationships between generic concepts of bowls and my specific, local and finite vocabulary of elements: bowl; tiles; pavers; water—or, circular and rectilinear forms. Questions about design strategies for a formalization of derivations and their semiotic relations emerged. It was a matter of

syntax rather than semantics to start with. This resulted in the following schematic system for the image development process.

1. **Vocabulary.** A set of elements was selected: bowl, bowl shadow, tile, tile join, paver, paver join, water.
2. **Rules.** Sets of rules between instances of the vocabulary were roughly postulated as follows:

Colour

1. If there is a colour—then it should be an average of the range of colours shown in a large area of the photograph.
2. If there are two colours—then their interaction should complement the entire image without dominance.
3. If there is a colour—then it is multicoloured at the edge.
4. If there is a colour—then it is not multicoloured at the edge (an alternative to rule 3).
5. If there is a colour—then the colour contains variety within the shape.
6. If colour is not in focus—then it needs an addition of complementary grey.

Composition

7. If the image has a central form—then it should contain some asymmetry.
8. If there is a shape—then it should have a harmonious relation with the entire framework.
9. If a there is a shape—then it should correspond to a dominant central vertical axis.
10. If there is a shape—then a variable grid pattern will guide arrangement.

11. If there is a focus—then a variety of sub-foci are needed to allow the eye to travel across and around the field.

Why the pot and the pool? The bowl has a significant history. A close friend made it during a period of rapid personal change in my life. The bowl carried both my pets and my food. My cat (Kobe) slept in it as a kitten. Our pet white doves (Jasper and Jesse) slept in it and often perched on its rim, watching us through the living room window during winter rains and hot blue summers. Cabbage salad was served from this special vessel for significant celebrations.

These tacit understandings of the role of objects in our lives stimulate the design endeavour. The pool was built using my design in 1994. It represents a union on several levels: within my personal relationship, within the sea and my place, within sky and water. The terracotta tiles were selected in deference to European-style architecture. The colours evoke travel memories and the work of De Chirico, Tuscany, Barcelona, Nice and Picasso's lifestyle legacy. It represents a chance to find the good life, to cherish the moods of the sea and sky—and to enjoy them by being in them.

When photographing the bowl, I was aware it was only a small and particular view, but I continued to explore it, to see what boundaries emerged: how far one could push a subject in different directions to find alternative but satisfactory solutions—but one might ask, solutions to what? For me, it was the problem of feeling the moment; the totality of a lifetime of looking; the experience of memory contained in the objects and the pleasures of colour, form, texture, light and shade; the perceptual epi-phenomena that result from the magic of a captured instant in time, a fragment of a life's inner visual sensation.

Looking back, it seems a revision of my personal visual vocabulary began with a new visual representation of my environment—just like learning a new language. Thinking in terms of rules and grammars revealed that my oeuvre could be extended and defined more clearly. Strategies inevitably arose for deciding what to keep.

Finding the most valuable kinds of rules became a key concern. Questions of grace, wit and elegance of rule sets were considered. I began to change my general assumptions about the design

Figure 8.7 *Bowl Series #1.*

Figure 8.8 *Bowl Series #2.*

Figure 8.9 *Bowl Series #3.*

Table 8.1   COMMENTS ON SOME OF THE IMAGES IN THE BOWL SERIES

Image	Comment
1	The first photograph is taken. A bowl placed on the side of a pool. The attitude is candid—a simple record shot to start. 'No tricky business!' David Dallwitz, my early mentor and later good friend, often teased us with this epithet to disarm our eager digital image-making experiments in composition and presentation. In my view, there is no innocent eye as the camera records only a selected slice of composed vision according to one's prejudice.
2	A few seconds later, the pool hose appears as a white line—I remove it; then add a deeper colour in the water; balance the shadows with a fragment from the other side of the pool; emphasise the horizontal band of terracotta. The shadows are too ordinary in arrangement. Perhaps a lack of the bowl's profile is an improvement.
3	What can be seen in a composition from the top? A much more powerful, simple and direct image—a half moon lit on the edge of the bowl, anonymity and universality, but still a particularity of my making. Memories arise: of bowls of cherries, grapes and pomegranates, in the art of Hamaguchi, a San Francisco artist's mezzotints my wife, Judith, and I encountered in 1983 on our first US trip. Still life—subject and image, related by presence and illusion, become a nebulous representational dialogue that matures into patterns of observation and analysis. Extraordinary and ordinary interweave as in Ben Nicholson's, Brancusi's or Jean Arp's work. A physical connection with objects is as important as the lessons of history.
4	Trying the shadow on the other side—or perhaps trying to move to the other side of the pool—what can be done with the shadows on the ledge of the pool? I link them with the bowl's shadow to give a sweeping movement in the foreground. Interesting composition results, but the view is too far away so that the composition appears too loose. The top water shape around the bowl is attractive. I prefer the bright half moon on the lower edge of the bowl. But is this a traditional view, inherited from all those standard primer diagrams in physics and photography classes where the light comes from the top left? Shadows have been a key consideration in all my work, but I had not formalized this aspect until this reflection on these images.
5	Close in—reveals a great shadow shape in the rear. Remove other distractions where possible. The diagonal angle of the edge of the pool seems uncomfortable. I sought a fusion of the camera's initial photograph and my subsequent imagination of an abstract composition.
6	Concerns are the shadow position, cropping of foreground and an unwelcome bright reflection on the rim of the bowl. Can a visual experience overwhelm one's inner reflection of a moment? A suspension of judgment while the experience was ingested through the camera led to a kind of blind optimism, an optimistic belief that a better solution was coming up. Design theorist Donald Norman discusses this apparent division between experience and reflection in his book *The Psychology of Everyday Things* (1988). It may be the reason why many artists are reluctant to discuss their work in print. Each time one returns to reflect, new associations and different ideas appear depending on what one brings to the viewing. A sense of grammar seems to guide the repetition of rule applications, but at this point in the process, the possibilities of future computer manipulations were concealed by the immediate photographic exploration. Awareness of the tension between loose schemas and the formal systems that computer software applies by default once the images are transferred to Photoshop or other computer image editing software.
23	The final image of this sequence (see Figure 8.11) considers whether the pool ledge shadow might be used in a more complicated way: 'Select and reject—look and put'—memories of South Australian painter and early mentor, Geoff Wilson's 1970s painting classes and discussions of Canaletto's selective simplification within his architectural paintings. The previous image is preferred because it is less complex and directs attention in and through the image with ambiguity and strength of purpose.

process through a growth in awareness of a search for rules and their various applications. The Bowl Series experiment marked a change in my general approach to form making that attempted to incorporate elements of previous attitudes and values while thinking about visual grammars. The following brief selected comments are based on the original reflective journal captured during the design process, supplemented by later thoughts.

I constructed a poster of the entire Bowl Series from a matrix of the individual images and their variations. It shows a compression of space and depicts the local coastal environment in micro-cosm. The view of the sea from a cliff top is a thrilling sensation because one knows one is high up. A depth of vision combined with a feeling of height adds a strange sensation to the experience of a cliff top environment, looking across and down at the same time. This sensation generated the composition in image 23 (see Figure 8.11), a turning point that revealed an alternative framing of spatial elements and consolidated the completion of this series of photographs.

To recap, formally the Bowl Series begins with the repetition of circular and rectangular shapes. The rectangular shapes are schematically layered or divided so that combinations of shapes may occur resulting in the systematic transformation of the circle.

Photoshop filters assist this derivation process (as in their application at the turning point where a grayscale system is used) with scaling and repetition rules. Colour systems are formally rule based in that they rely upon the Photoshop set of colours used by the computer system or printer.

As in the experiments with tonal scales, extremes of each colour variable (for example, contrast, brightness, hue, saturation and reversal) are altered.

Figure 8.10 *Bowl Series #4, 5, 6.*

Figure 8.11 *Bowl Series #23.*

Figure 8.12 *Ceramic Bowl,* Marianne Cole, 1993.

Pattern recognition

A contingent sense of pattern and consciousness of visual grammar is clearly dominant in these works. Emergent strategies evolved such as the move from a general to a close-up view, reduction in scale and repetition of elements. This dynamic corresponds with a formal move from photographic representation towards abstract pattern; from colour to black and white; from static conventional depiction of space to a more dynamic, repetitive optical illusion based on black-and-white contrast.

Turning points

Changes in the grammar can be seen in the changes of the vocabulary elements. Photographic elements change to abstract elements in the key turning point of image 25, which was loosely traced over a photographic image. Other turning points may be found in the following images which changed the grammar through vocabulary alteration and rule transformation (see Figure 8.5).

Image	Comment
3	Standard to top view
24	Colour to black and white
25	Photographic elements change to abstract elements
35	Photographic to hand-drawn shapes
42	Regular to distortion filters
49	Scaling down and repetition

In his analysis of multimedia in the design studio, Richard Coyne argues, 'computers certainly make a difference. If that difference is not simply better and more efficient design, then what is the difference?' (1996).

The Bowl Series reflects an iterative pattern of rule selection. This sequence invites intervention and subsequent reapplication of rule(s). Moments of insight and points of change are recognized through reflection on these form-making experiments. The ubiquitous role of schemas (emerging grammars) and formal grammatical visual systems in the design derivation process demonstrates that grammars can be used contingently in particular contexts such as art, and that they may be changed and switched contingently.

The next example offers insights into the three-dimensional application of a grammatical view of design to architectural design.

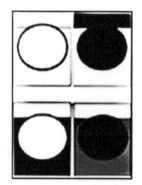 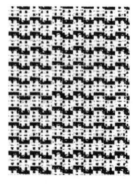

Figure 8.13 *Bowl Series #48, 49, 54.*

example 2: *Workday Weekenders* (Tony)

I have worked as an architect and a planner, but I teach and do research and have not built much for many years. This pair of houses was built in Adelaide, Australia, with the intention that my wife and I would live in one of the pair and our student daughters in the other.[1] The name comes from the idea of having a home to return to at the end of every working day that has the relaxed, informal feel of a weekender holiday house.

I often begin by making a digital model of the site and the neighbouring buildings. The model does not need to be highly accurate, just enough to provide a context for exploring design options. With this digital model I can zoom in to focus on design details, and then out to see the resulting urban form. I can also use the same model to investigate sun and shade and views. Often, I make a physical cardboard model as well; both models have different and complimentary characteristics. I can pick up a physical model and turn it around and move my eye from detail to big picture with more immediacy than with a digital model, but it is laborious to model surface qualities and I cannot put myself inside as I can with a digital model. 3D digital experiences partially bridge the gap between digital and physical, but I will still use both.

The houses were to be constructed on an empty site in a row of single storey cottages; a similar cottage had once stood there, but it had been demolished before we arrived. A building's first duty is to its neighbours. Most art (painting and sculpture) is created without reference to the specific location of its installation. Most artists know nothing of the wall or place that their work will be displayed. Like environmental and installation art, however, site and place is fundamental to architecture.

Figure 8.14 *Workday Weekender* houses, 2001–4. Antony Radford.

Patterns

I began with some patterns that I wanted to adapt. Both houses were to allow privacy for guests or children separate from the main part of the house, along the general pattern of a long, thin house with numerous courtyards set out in the book *Community and Privacy* by Serge Chermayeff and Christopher Alexander (1963).

This pattern was overlaid by the traditional three-floor cottage pattern with a main floor, attic and cellar. There were also precedents of houses designed by other architects, particularly the Thiel House designed by Troppo Architects in Darwin, Australia, and the Hammond House

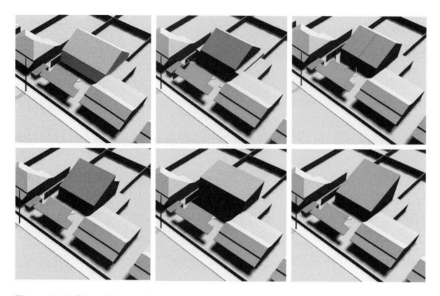

Figure 8.15 Six studies of building form. Antony Radford.

in Pomona, Australia, designed by Lindsay and Kerry Claire.[2]

Vocabulary

The vocabulary of the neighbouring cottages was stone or rendered rectangular blocks with low-pitched corrugated iron roofs and front verandahs, a very typical building form for the late nineteenth century in Adelaide. It is evocative of history, tradition and domesticity. On the other side of the road, a row of two-storey brick apartments had been built in the 1960s. This is a bigger mass with little subtlety in form. It is evocative of close living, of minimal concern with decoration or articulation in design. None of these buildings was designed by architects. Along with these sources from the site, there were some additional influences on my choice of vocabulary. I have a fondness for galvanized corrugated iron, its texture, repetitive module, weathering and colour. It begins life as a shiny, reflective metal, weathers to a dull grey of varied tones, and eventually in

old age takes on colours of deep pinks and reds as it begins to rust (sadly it also begins to leak). Light plays over its corrugated surface to produce stripes of shade and brightness. Like stone and timber, it weathers gracefully. I am also fond of timber, with its grain and texture and easy ability to be shaped. This combination of corrugated iron and timber can be found in innumerable old Australian buildings.

In a previous house, a mezzanine upper level overlooked a room below at one end, and kicked out at the other end to a roof window. Standing on the mezzanine at one point, then, I could look down into the lower room, while further along on the same side I could look out of the roof window. I liked this. It seemed that the L in this mezzanine edge could be replaced by a \, a diagonal line that left a space under the sloping roof at one end and almost met it at the other end.

The initial vocabulary, then, was a carport on the street side acting as a surrogate verandah; double-pitched, corrugated steel roofs to match

Figure 8.16 Key ideas, shown for the left-hand house: (a) A long, thin site where the sun will shine on the back of the house. (b) Divide the site into building and courtyard zones. (c) Slope roofs away from courtyards so the sky is visible . . . (d) But add sunshades to protect the walls in summer. (e) Make a diagonal edge to the upper floor to allow views out through a roof window and down to the main floor. (f) There are three built elements. (g) On one side place a brick spine wall to provide sound and fire separation between this house and its neighbour. (h) On the other side of the house insert translucent wall panels. (i) Split the roof over the front built element to match the verandahs on neighbouring houses. (j) Dig a small cellar under the house. (k) Raise the entry side of the main house to be between the main and upper levels. (l) Locate the main living space next to the largest courtyard. The three smaller spaces can be sleeping or work rooms. (m) At the back of the house insert a diagonal mirror to give a reflected view of the courtyard when looking down the length of the house. (n) There are views out to courtyards or the street from every room. (o) The external form of the house. It is repeated and reflected for the right-hand house.

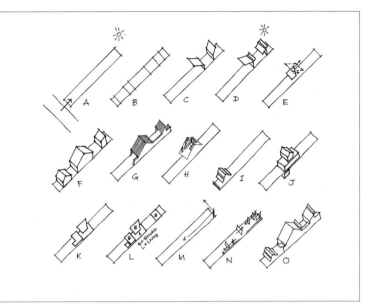

the other cottages in the street; corrugated iron side walls; coloured, textured front and back walls; an angled mezzanine edge to the attic floor; a cellar and an attic; a brick spine wall; sun shades on the north façades.

Rules

The verandahs of the existing cottages on the same side of the street form a line about 2 metres (6 ft) back from their front fences. They had been built before cars and car parking; some had space for a car beside the house, others had no space. The need for off-street parking (a Council requirement) meant that the new houses would have to be pushed farther back from the street to allow for parking in front. The initial rules were these:

1. Position the carport to line up with neighbouring verandahs, and thereby provide continuity in the streetscape.
2. Concentrate space in one big room.
3. Allow a room to appropriate space from a neighbouring larger room (or the exterior) through openings.
4. Make divisions between rooms as sliding screens that look in place when open, rather than as hinged doors.
5. Allow daylight into the interior.
6. Make materials selectively visible: plywood, timber beams, corrugated iron, and bolted connections.[3]
7. Make detailing simple and straightforward to build.

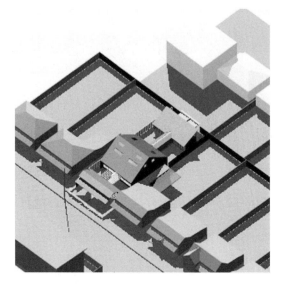

Figure 8.17 Key ideas combined in a digital model of the two houses. Antony Radford.

Derivation of the design

One of the problems of architecture is that there is rarely an opportunity to build a prototype before the final version. Building a digital virtual prototype is at least a partial substitute. The process I followed was to begin with a hand-sketched plan that explored the planning possibilities of the site, and then moved very quickly to 3D digital modelling to explore the resulting massing in the context of the site and its neighbours. The vocabulary could then be tested in the 3D model, trying different possibilities.

In the first developed version of the project, I proposed to build to the boundary at both sides, maximizing the use of a narrow site (6 metres or 18 ft for each house). This, though, precluded the translucency at one side that I sought for the main room of the house; it also created a difficult construction situation where one of the two houses would have abutted a neighbouring cottage. The second version, therefore, kept construction away from the boundaries, allowing for a band of translucent wall lights along the sides. These were strips of corrugated polycarbonate sheet inserted in a wall clad in horizontal corrugated galvanized iron, the whole being more like a roof on its side than a conventional wall.

The constructed houses echo their digital predecessors, although there has been a continual refinement of detail to simplify building and promote consistency — or simply to respond to unexpected contingencies. In every new detail there is a strong sense of how it needs to be to fit with the language that has been established by earlier details. It is a house where the construction can be read from its form and those selective areas of missing linings where the underlying elements show through. It is a highly grammatical house, with a grammar that is robust enough to cope with the variations that occur on site.

These houses were designed and built without using BIM (building information modelling), with no complex free-form curving surfaces and only a small amount of CNC fabrication (for the stairs and for some of the steelwork). Looking ahead, even this kind of small-scale building will routinely use BIM and CAD-CAM processes. Whether the design media will need to cope with free-form curving surfaces will depend on the designers' choices, but the media opens up choices that used to be impracticable.

The next example offers insights into the application of a grammatical view of design to two-dimensional serial imagery.

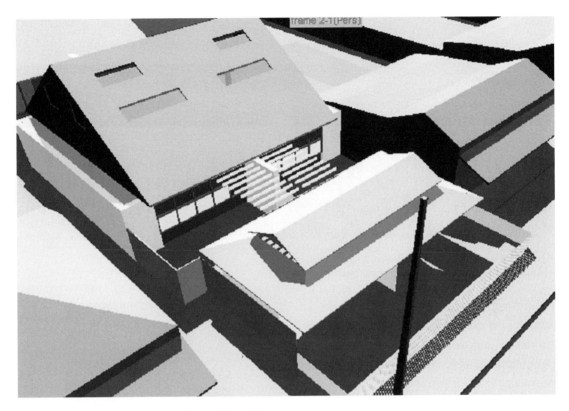

Figure 8.18 *Workday Weekender* design model exploring roof options. Antony Radford.

example 3: two-dimensional serial #*panoramas*+ (Dean)

The #*panoramas*+ *Series* experimented with the relatively formal application of a grammatical approach to two-dimensional digital imaging to extend sequential notions of abstraction. These serial works are all digital derivations of panoramic photographs. They explored some Australian coastal environments using abstraction within a structured set of self-imposed rules. The experience provided insights into the contingent nature of image making (in spite of the intention to follow rules) and the power of digital abstraction to evoke a sense of the poetic.

The conceptual underpinning of these digital media works was founded on several coincident current discourses in new media. The imagery embraces aspects of generative design theory with notions such as lexicon, rules and operations whilst, by contrast, questioning the nature of post-structuralist spatial understanding. Through explorative alternative understandings of time and place, notions of complexity, truth and visual identity are interwoven in the panoramic image manipulation.

The series embraces ideas of expressionism and the idea that local becomes global. Formally, these compositions explore the contradiction between apparent depth and compositional flatness

Figure 8.19 *#panoramas+ Series*, *Maslin*, 2003, the first and the last images of the series. Courtesy of Dean Bruton.

in a picture space. They revel in the colours and forms of the panorama in a poetic colourist interpretation but also consciously follow a grammatical protocol of vocabulary, patterns, rules and derivations in the design language.

Vocabulary

I selected the vocabulary within a reductionist framework that intentionally limited the possible outcomes. The imagery was grounded in events of personal significance. It explores South Australia's Fleurieu Peninsula's coastal views and walking trails, and the urban interiors of shops and private homes, seen through a grammatical lens.

1. A panoramic photographic image constructed from a set of five to ten images.
2. Three-dimensional views of the landscape juxtaposed against two-dimensional formats.
3. Digital brush strokes, between three and ten pixels wide.
4. Colour palettes based on each panoramic image's colour scheme.

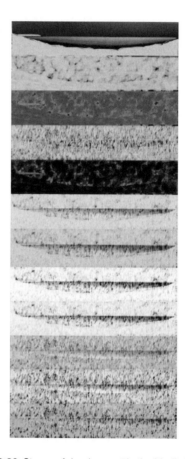

Figure 8.20 Stages of development in the *Maslin* imagery, from *#panoramas+ Series*, 2003.

Rules and derivations

Rules provide starting points (not ends in themselves), with contingency always present and influential. The sequence starts with a photograph and then offers abstract variations on the original image according to a set of rules that are often interrupted by contingent decisions.

1. Capture photographic digital images in overlapping sequences suitable for assemblage on a computer using panoramic construction software.
2. Open the panoramic image in Photoshop or similar desktop image editing software.
3. Use hand-drawn digital brush strokes to simplify and abstract the composition.
4. Represent the overall composition as flat areas of shape.
5. Redefine the surface of the image using overlapping brush strokes.
6. Use an electronic tablet and digital drawing stylus.
7. Develop a series of images using the fifth, tenth or fifteenth iteration as a completion point.
8. Transform the photorealistic illusion to brush marks.
9. Develop a colour scheme based on colour sampling of the original panoramic image.
10. Construct a harmonious, rhythmic composition that finds a satisfying balance of forms and colour.
11. Use a bleed device with overlapping colours at edges.
12. Construct a new layer for each derivation.

Each work was presented as a series of form and colour derivations originally based on horizontal panoramic digital images. The final selection varied in size according to the contingencies of cropping and scale. The first in the series was developed using the idea that there would be only ten variations. This became difficult because the image often seemed to need another layer to be completed. The system broke down to include sequential variations other than those in groups of five, ten and fifteen. An exhibition in 2003 selected ten sequences for public display. The first image (panoramic photograph) and the last image (abstract digital derivation) in each series were hung together. This series of works gave an insight into the relative ease of digital media production informed by a grammatical approach to form making. It aims to evoke a sense of place in a poetic fashion through revisions of the image, reflected in the writing of Paul Valéry.

This quiet roof, where dove-sails saunter by,
Between the pines, the tombs, throbs visibly.
Impartial noon patterns the sea in flame—
That sea forever starting and re-starting.
When thought has had its hour, oh how
    rewarding
Are the long vistas of celestial calm! (From 'The
    Graveyard by the Sea', 1920 by Paul Valéry,
    translated by Cecil Day-Lewis; Valéry 1922)

The next example offers a grammatical view of graphic design.

example 4: *Workday Weekenders* poster (Tony)

Entering the *Workday Weekenders* in the state architecture awards scheme (successfully) necessitated the design of an A1 poster. My methodology

Figure 8.21 Stages in the development of the *Workday Weekenders* poster from early concept (top left) to final version (bottom right). Courtesy of Antony Radford.

was to make low resolution copies of suitable photographs and play with these in trying out possibilities on a low resolution A1 background, using Photoshop. Only when the design was complete and stable were these images replaced by higher resolution versions suitable for printing. I could have used software specifically intended for designing posters and similar graphic design products, but I had Photoshop on my laptop and that was fine.

The starting point was to adopt a pattern common for such posters: a large hero image of the exterior that would dominate the poster and be read from a distance, supported by a smaller image of an interior, and both of these supplemented by a selection of further small images on an underlying grid. The poster grammar would be a vocabulary of rectangular images on a white background where the smaller images were clustered. The regularity of this composition was interrupted by two contingencies: a desire to align the back of the building above the hero image of the front, so that this small picture could not be a part of the small image cluster, and the desire to include a plan drawing that did not easily fit into the rectangular image format. This led to a new rule that the centre line of the pair of houses would be located on the same vertical line on the poster, aligning the front, rear and plan images.

Playing with the image sizes and positions led to the insertion of two views of the main interior above the hero image. The larger of these includes the centre wall of the houses, and is thus aligned according to the rule noted previously on the same key vertical line as the back and front views and the plan. An additional rule limits text to single lines at the extreme top and bottom of the poster.

An experiment introduced three new organizing rules. The first placed all images of the upper floor, along with the plan of the upper floor, on the left-hand side of the poster. This inevitably and finally broke the cluster small images rule, which was then discarded. The second ordered the images of the ground floor so that the entry (southern) image was placed at the bottom of the poster, and other images placed in order with the far (northern) exterior at the top of the poster. This moved the hero image to the bottom. The third new rule was to place photographs close to the relevant part of the plan. This rule meant that the plan had to be enlarged and the rule to align the centre wall along the same vertical line in the poster had to be bent, so that the main interior view that included this wall could be moved

outside the plan. The underlying organizing grid was weakened and frequently broken. Indeed, one image—looking down from the upper level to the ground floor—was superimposed in the appropriate place on the plan itself, where it remained throughout further development of the layout.

Reflecting on this version of the poster suggested that the main organizing rule become one of the poster telling a story about movement through the building, with the plan and photographs that illustrated parts of the plan becoming more important than the original hero image, which was reduced in size. There then needed to be some compensating device for providing the distant impact, when the poster is too far away from the viewer for the detail of the plan or photographs to be seen. This was achieved by bending the white background rule. Instead of white, this would be a grayscale version of the rear view of the building, enlarged to fill the whole poster. The other vocabulary elements were superimposed on this background. The organizing grid for arranging the edges and sizes of images was re-empowered, although still bent in places.

The final version of the poster kept all of these rules. The grayscale background rule, though, was bent to allow colour on two small sections of visible wall, differentiating the two houses. The plan was made transparent to allow the background image more visibility, and a colour coding of the plan to indicate different levels (cellar, ground and upper floors) was introduced. The text line rule was also bent to allow more information about the house and those involved in its construction to be included.

Through this sequence of imposing, bending and sometimes abandoning rules, the composition of the poster developed. However, this was never only an issue of graphic design. The patterns and grammar were mobilized in an endeavour to tell a story about the building in a clear and succinct way.

The next example offers insights into the application of grammatical view of design to installation art.

example 5: SEQ series— three-dimensional modelling and animation (Dean)

For architectural form making and sculptural exploration for installation art, early solid modelling applications such as Form Z, Strata Studio Pro, Maya and 3D Studio Max were exciting. The challenge was to interpret ideas within the grammatical rules of a 3D modelling program. Divorcing an art work's form from its content is problematic. All art has some kind of semantic aim, and my work is no exception. Even with the emphasis on form making, an idea drives the key direction of the work.

The ideas behind the SEQ series are explained in the next section in terms of grammatical design in three dimensions. Generative design software such as John Maeda's *Processing* and Ceccato's 2008 *Origine* later challenged this kind of form making.

The SEQ series explored time sequences to develop threads of earlier post-structuralist themes using ready-made digital objects. These objects were found online in the same way that Duchamp may have found his famous urinal. Everyday objects were selected in a whimsical way, objects such as a cubic crate, lamp, augur and pocket watch for experiments in time and spatial montage.

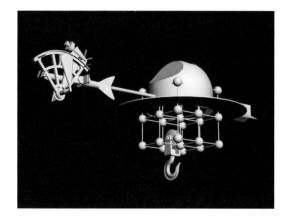

Figure 8.22 *SEQ#1*, computer graphic on canvas. Courtesy of Dean Bruton.

My work was directly personal and intentionally grammatical in that a conscious decision was made to limit the number of objects and the rules for the depiction of their interaction in time and space.

SEQ#1 was a response to the 2002 start of war in Iraq. As the oil wells burned on the TV news, the images of a colourless world seemed appropriate as an expression of the mood of the times. I chose a hat thinking of George Bush and Texan cowboy culture, a sextant thinking of finding a way for the new world order, an arrow as a reminder of the dual nature of conflict and a need to resolve conflict to find peace, a molecular array as a way of enframing all things and a gantry hook as a means of connection with the unknown. Others may attribute different symbolic meanings to these objects, but I record these thoughts here to illustrate the dialogue between ideas in time and form making.

When exhibited together as part of the 2003 Graphite Conference, at the Span Galleries in Melbourne, the exchange between the still images on the wall and the moving image projections referenced the changes in my own move from painting to digital media.

Rules and derivations

SEQ#2 and *SEQ#3* followed the same sequence of development with five different vocabulary objects and spatial considerations. The rules were intentionally simple:

Choose five objects at random from the stock supply of mesh vocabularies.

Arrange the objects in close proximity.

Adjust the position of the objects to construct a composition for a still image.

Animate the objects by adding them one at a time to a scene.

Use the black background as a compositional element.

Create a movie using a single camera that moves upwards vertically in a spiral.

Light the scene so that all objects are visible and distinctly recognizable.

SEQ#2 explored the idea of enframing and framing objects, and used associations of unlimited space beyond the frame, as in the well-known example of the looking glass in Lewis Carroll's *Alice in Wonderland.* A close-up view offered a refreshing compositional variation. A switching or replacement rule was applied in the middle of the series development. Changing the background from white to black seemed consistent with the original mood and semantic intent of the series. Developing a semantic link beyond the simply formalist constructions prompted *SEQ#3*.

SEQ#3 refers to a famous quote from the surrealist Isidore Ducasse: 'As curious as a chance encounter between a sewing machine and an umbrella on an ironing board in an operating theatre'.

The arrangement of these objects was based on an attempt to balance the objects and the

Figure 8.23 *SEQ#2,* computer graphic on canvas.
Courtesy of Dean Bruton.

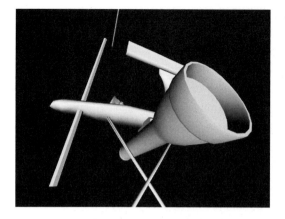

Figure 8.24 *SEQ#3*, computer graphic on canvas. Courtesy of Dean Bruton.

background so that neither dominated whilst creating an interesting composition for the journey of the eye—attention to the entry and exit points and the dynamic paths within the formal arrangement of objects.

SEQ#4 attempted to exaggerate the feeling of a deep spatial divide by contrasting the stable crate with the lamp base. Once the objects were

animated, a new set of relationships emerged between the sound track, objects, background and camera.

SEQ#5, the last in the series, extended this direction by choosing long, thin objects to maximize the blackness and ambiguity of the background. *SEQ#5* explored time sequences to develop threads of earlier post-structuralist themes using ready-made digital objects such as a cubic crate, lamp, augur and pocket watch in the Duchampian tradition.

Animation

Experiments continued in conjunction with the construction of a sound track for a series of short movies. The sound track rules were also simple enough to allow a cohesive mood to be developed by using a deep meditative, sonorous tone similar to those I had heard on my travels through Japan to the monasteries in Osaka. The sound track was applied to each of the five movies to unify the sequence and to evoke a kind of mandala in digital media. For the practitioner, multimedia and electronic publishing media are continually developing stages of refinement. The gallery space constrained the display and movie presentation possibilities. The movies were projected on the west wall amidst the still images on the other walls to present a compelling dialogue.

The idea of a prime language, of working towards a fundamental personal vision, permeates these works, but the grammatical rule base drives the formal compositions to a large extent. Contingency plays a role despite the efforts to maintain a formal approach.

Our final example is a video commission.

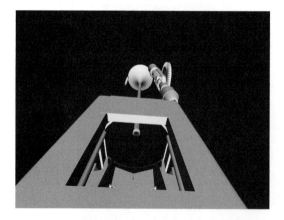

Figure 8.25 *SEQ#4*, computer graphic on canvas. Courtesy of Dean Bruton.

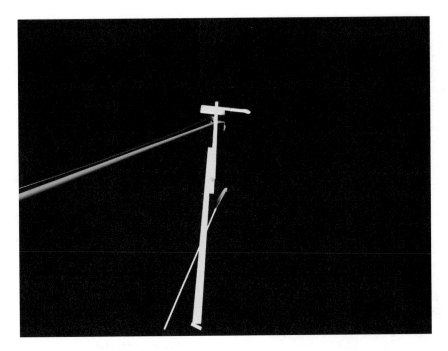

Figure 8.26 *SEQ#5*, computer graphic on canvas.
Courtesy of Dean Bruton.

example 6: designing a music video for broadcast television (Dean)

This project began when a group of five young musicians, the Shiny Brights, approached me to design a video for their new song called 'Take No More'. The project was to be done in two weeks for the budding group's forthcoming publicity campaign. After meeting key group members, some initial rules were set. These rules were very broad, such as 'Do doodles' and 'We want the words to be used in the imagery.' The general idea was to use video footage of the group making music against a backdrop of doodles. Beyond this, I had a free hand.

Developing a vocabulary

First ideas were developed by asking questions about intolerable situations, such as whaling, deforestation, global warming, war, disease, lies and injustice, hunger and poverty. These semantic nodes were quickly depicted in sketchy iconographic form, and thus began a new visual language used in the music video. At a Japanese restaurant I made sketches for additional vocabulary elements on a handy brochure from the local mobile phone stand: Mayo patterns inspired by the okonomiyaki pancake, hand-drawn marks that developed a colour pattern, the pattern of a rotating ceiling fan shadow, glows that echoed the music dynamics and vertical bars that related to the timeline and beat of the music.

Figure 8.27 *Take No More*, music video stills, the Shiny Brights, 2010. Courtesy of Dean Bruton.

Using rules

Finding a method of associating the core ideas is always a major part of composition. In this case, the five musicians were keen to distinguish their unique instrumental roles within the band. A schematic was designed that related the five shiny bright lights to the earth, the mother of all shiny brights. The idea brought in sketches of each instrument used in the band, such as drums, guitar and voice. The song was 3.5 minutes long and the climax was at the 2.33 minutes mark. The aim was to introduce the instruments, relate them to the song's text with associated imagery and then create a dynamic colour event to transition into the song's climax and lead into an interesting visual ending.

Identifying patterns

I needed to find a way to visually represent the semantic concerns of the song. The following chart was developed to help instil consistency and bring together these early ideas.

Element	Concern
Clock time	running out before chaos
Empty bowl	poverty
Whales	anti-whaling
Cut trees	deforestation
Cloud/sun	global warming
Rockets	war
Flying machines	oil crisis
Fan	grim reaper

The band members encouraged the doodle-style drawings once they could see the animation process at work. The flying machines and rockets were added. The empty bowl became symbolic of hunger and poverty, and endorsed the use of other circular patterns in the vocabulary.

Interventions and constraints

After a preliminary draft viewing, the group endorsed the approach but wanted more emphasis on the band as a band, despite the decision not to use instruments in the video component. Annotated lyrics and emphasis became the leading concerns, prompting editing of the length of various sections. The whaling section and the deforestation sections were reduced in time and dominance. The addition of a girl in distress was required to emphasize the conventional interpretation of the song as a romantic scenario in crisis. In a vague but ordered approach, a series of schematic rules for the final production could then be devised:

- Movement of shapes to emulate a lift or elevator
- Dust and particles to be added throughout
- Vertical bars to run periodically through the scene
- Squiggles, scrolls and doodles to feature as transitional elements
- Flying machine doodles punctuate the abstraction with figuration
- Folding shapes to introduce major changes in the score
- Glows to feature at specific points in the sound track
- Digital clock to feature as a time icon
- Band members' names to be used and song text to be used
- Whale bones to magically emerge as directional movement for the eye

Some of these rules were eventually edited to make way for the core ideas to be emphasized in the final production. Once these ideas emerged from the dialogue, the drawings and animations

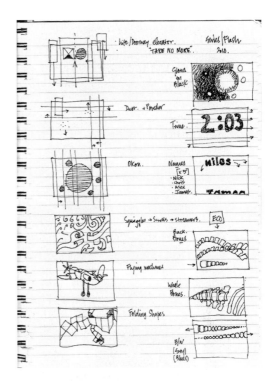

Figure 8.28 Shiny Brights, *Take No More*, music video, visual vocabulary elements in first idea sketches, 2010. Courtesy of Dean Bruton.

Figure 8.29 *Take No More*, music video test animation composite sequence. Courtesy of Dean Bruton.

Figure 8.30 *Take No More*, music video featuring rock group the Shiny Brights, screened on *Rage*, ABC television broadcast. Courtesy of Dean Bruton.

were developed in Flash and After Effects. These were combined with the video footage, checked with the group and output to various formats for delivery online and for broadcast television. The result was spectacular success according to the group. It was launched on MySpace and screened on YouTube. A popular music video program on Australian ABC television, *Rage*, made the song feature of the week and it was screened many times in May 2010, to the delight of the band and its fans.

This two-week project served to highlight the advantages of thinking within a grammatical

mindset to constrain possibilities and develop alternatives as much as possible to meet a strict deadline and client expectations. The final outcome reminded me that art and commerce often have different expectations that shape the final product.

We have framed these six examples as demonstrations that we use concepts of rules, grammar, patterns and contingency in a practical way in our own work. They serve as case studies of grammatical design practice. There is another way of looking at these examples, and that is as an essential part of our own research on and growing understanding of the role and interaction of these concepts. Indeed, it is inherent in reflective practice that any practice is potentially a part of a personal research program, generating new knowledge of personal or wider significance.

In this enterprise of design and art as research, there are issues that can be explored that are much harder to investigate in other ways. Reading reports of the research of others or analysing the designs or artworks of others does not provide the immediacy of engagement with situations that analysing our own work provides. Especially, it does not highlight the contingencies, the way (in our cases) that our grammatical agenda is disturbed by other agendas in our work or by the unexpected events in the story of design development: the way sunlight falls on a bowl when taking a photograph, the way a builder misinterprets a drawing, the way a spontaneous mark contributes to a composition, the way the colour printing turns out on a poster, the way an art installation is performed, the reaction of a music band to the initial screening of a video. The practice of design and art throws up these contingencies and provides the necessity and context for inventing ways to deal with them. This would be a very different book without the experience of our own designing.

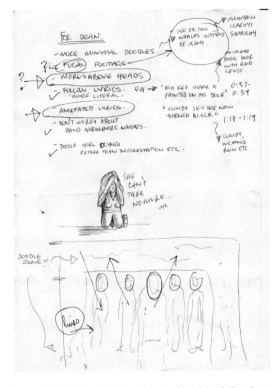

Figure 8.31 Client feedback sheet with minimal directions for the music video *Take No More*. Courtesy of Dean Bruton.

Summary: On Personal Projects

Our awareness and interest in rules and the effects of contingency, the need to bend the rules, is deeply influential in the way we design. Understanding more about this influence is a continuing personal project.

chapter 9

critical ideas

This brief book on design can be no more than an introduction, and we hope readers will follow it with more reading about and (more importantly) doing digital design. We end this book by briefly recapitulating its key critical ideas, and looking forwards.

from the preceding chapters, what are the critical ideas to guide our work?

There are compelling reasons why design should be based on the use of digital media, and these reasons extend across many design fields. Given this context, as designers we need to think and work in ways that recognize and exploit the characteristics of digital media. Being clearly, consistently and overtly aware of patterns and grammars in design within a frame of mind that accepts and welcomes contingency can assist creativity and the development of design confidence and skill. We can link systematic and intuitive thinking. There is nothing magical or surprising in this. If we look at what in the past has been acclaimed as great art and design, we find just this linking of recurrent patterns and strong, consistent grammar with an openness and adaptation to inevitable contingency. We argue that the embedding of patterns and rules in the software of contemporary digital media makes this even more important than it has been in the past.

That does not make design easy.[1] Design is an effort as well as a delight. The architect Edwin Lutyens spoke of wrestling with the language of classical architecture, a choice of word that expresses both struggle and play. It is always easier to take the obvious options. We need to be both determined and confident if we are to feel free to take risks and break boundaries, to think forbidden thoughts.

In each chapter of this book we have sought to answer a question related to the development of digital design awareness and understanding.

What are the rules in digital design?

Designers typically respond to design opportunities by using patterns and following rules that seem to fit the situation. The most common source of these patterns and rules is their own previous work. But these patterns and rules are not immutable things that reduce designing to the routine following of predetermined prescriptions. Instead, they are starting points rather than answers, and always need interpretation in the specific context of their use. In digital design, the designer's rules are accompanied by the media's rules, and the two sets must be compatible.

How does contingency intervene in the operation of rules?

Contingency permeates every design activity. It prompts designers to adapt or abandon common patterns and rules and to seek out new and less obvious ones, adding to the designer's personal store for future reference. Using digital media tends to inhibit ambiguity in design descriptions and the emergence of new interpretations that easily arise with ambiguous descriptions. But using digital media also tends to encourage the exploration of alternatives and through parametric design allows outcomes to adapt to different contexts.

How do rules and contingency interplay in different kinds of digital design?

Rules and contingency interplay in all fields of design. There is always interplay between following the rules of existing patterns and grammars and adapting to contingencies. Looking at art and design in terms of rules and grammar can never be objective and independent, let alone all-encompassing, but it does provide something of a lingua franca for cross-discipline and cross-cultural discourse. Looking at the rules and grammar in one design field can enrich our understanding and endeavours in another field.

Can we be more creative with digital design?

Seeking creativity is a choice. It can be facilitated by being aware that patterns and rules can both empower and limit, and by seeking in a practical but relaxed way to welcome and adapt to the demands of contingency. We should always be open to the possibility of change, contingently adapting or even radically recasting the patterns and rules we are using. Moments of change—of disruption—in our design rules and vocabulary are significant moments of inspiration and redirection.

What can we learn from precedents in product design, art, architecture, film and games?

The work that those who are recognized as both highly creative and highly productive in all of these fields exhibits the very strong development of

consistent personal grammars—and periodic, apparently disruptive but ultimately productive changes in those grammars. If we examine collections of such work, we find consistency (the repetitive use of variations of patterns and grammars), development (the gradual evolution of new patterns and grammars) and instances of minor or sometimes radical change in response to contingencies.

How can we develop digital skills and creativity through play?

We develop our skills and knowledge by doing, by experiencing the reflective practice that underlies design. In play, we can combine the processes of learning about software and learning about designing using the software. We need the confidence and competence to express our ideas fluently, and much digital design software is complex for the beginner. Discovering how to design with the software, not working through manuals, best develops this capability. Clarity about rules and vocabulary makes it easier. This does not mean that other ways of looking at design need to be rejected or downplayed; design can be a game with multiple agendas.

What is the interplay of rules and contingency in our own designs?

Keeping a journal helps reveal the patterns and grammars we have consciously or unconsciously used, and how contingency has affected our work. Designers throughout history have kept journals or notebooks. Make a note of ideas and patterns as they appear, and keep a digital file of part-completed designs.

Designs are not necessarily better because of the media used: *Citizen Kane*, the Cylinda-Line and Espansiva houses are all pre-digital but have lasting value. Digital art is not always better than a charcoal sketch, nor is digital architecture always better than a hand-crafted vernacular hut. They have different qualities. We have drawn attention to some of the reasons why digital design is dominant: collaboration in a world of convergent digital communication; the digital work flow, from first idea to production; the advantages of digital prototypes and the prediction of their performance; the re-use of digital patterns and procedures; the generation of alternatives; the way a digital image can simulate the appearance of the physical world and communicate ideas to others. There is a lot of designing to do, to enrich the lives of others and to meet environmental and social challenges. As designers we respond as best we can with the most appropriate media.

We advocate this: look at the world with grammatical eyes. Analyse trees and plants, household objects, buildings and art asking, what are the patterns, what is the vocabulary, what are the rules, what is the grammar? Analyse digital artefacts such as Web sites, film and games in the same way. In your own work, ask yourself this: 'What is the grammar of this work?' And look for telltale signs of the impact of contingency: the way a plant adapts its structure to seek light, the way a design deals with its context. Then be open to change in your own designing, welcoming and adapting to the inevitable intrusion of contingency.

Summary: Digital Design Is Not Mysterious

The activities involved are the same as those in other human activities: we follow patterns, we follow rules, and we try to make what we do purposeful and meaningful and to make sense of it as a whole. We develop our own ways of doing things, our own vocabulary and grammar. Most of the time all of this is fairly obvious, and the design outcomes fairly obvious. Sometimes we designers take rare patterns, bend the rules, find endpoints outside expectations and create something that is exceptional which excites others and ourselves.

notes

_____

chapter 1: rules and digital design

1. For example, by 2010 the average UK resident spent just over seven hours a day looking at/listening to/using media (statistics from Ofcom, the UK regulator for TV, radio and telecommunications at http://www.bbc.co.uk/news/technology-11012356, accessed 22 Aug. 2010).

2. For a comprehensive review of the literature and approaches to design in the digital age, see the special issue of _Design Studies_ on digital design (Oxman 2006a and particularly Oxman 2006b).

3. See, for example, philosopher Stanley Fish's observation that we 'will always be guided by the rules or rules of thumb that are the content of any settled practice' (1985: 106).

4. Computer simulation of plants using L-systems is described in the book _The Algorithmic Beauty of Plants_ (Prusinkiewicz and Lindenmayer 1990). L-system (named after their developer biologist Aristid Lindenmayer) is a kind of formal grammar that can generate self-similar fractal forms.

5. In this book, we use the terms _grammar_, _vocabulary_ and _language_ in the usual way, as metaphors. This is important to make clear because in one branch of research, shape grammars, these words have acquired very specific meanings. From the 1960s, a discourse developed that draws on linguist Noam Chomsky's work on the formalization of grammar in written and spoken language.

Designs derived from a properly specified rule system, a grammar, constitute a language. Transformations of rules provide a translation from one language to another. (March and Stiny 1985: 31)

By studying, using and writing particular shape grammars, underlying rules are made manifest. George Stiny depicts such grammars as computationally open for exploration (2006), a tool for art and design in making the judgemental process more transparent.

6. Stiny asserts in his book _Shape_ that 'there is no vocabulary. Design is more than combining units whatever they are' (2006: 393). While agreeing that 'design is more than combining units' and a defined vocabulary inhibits the perception of emergent form (see Chapter 2), we remain convinced of the value of thinking in terms of both rules and vocabularies in digital design.

7. Russell Kirsch was one of the first to develop the idea that pictures could be represented grammatically using computers (Kirsch 1964). In a later interview with Joan Kirsch, the two authors explained the development this way:

The original idea for this occurred quite a long time ago, in the early 1960s, when we were all doing work in mathematical translation of languages. People were very excited about the notion of writing grammars for language. This was the first attempt, growing out of Noam Chomsky's work, to be formal about a language that all the computational linguistics people were using. For such work as this, I was one of the fortunate people who had the use of SEAC, the only powerful computer around, which we had built originally at the National Bureau of Standards. It was the first of the contemporary computers in this country.

I thought that it would be interesting to see whether you could extend this notion of language to describe images. So I wrote, for the SEAC, what was probably the first picture grammar with regular productions operating on rectilinear arrays of symbols and generated a simple class of images like triangles. That notion caught on and it became a little sub field called picture syntax in the pattern recognition community devoted to writing grammars. (Kirsch and Kirsch 1996)

In the 1960s, Russell Kirsch had concluded that these grammars ('descriptive theories' in the words used at the time) for text and picture languages could be used by computers to 'analyse individual information items at a purely syntactic (formal) level', but he noted that it 'is tempting to identify these interpretation operations with the informal notion of "understanding"' (1964: 376). It is almost impossible to see or hear any design (art, architecture, music or dance) without it suggesting meanings in our minds.

8. These can be generated using Stephen Linhart's Web site for Mondrimat, http://www. stephen.com/mondrimat/, accessed 28 Apr. 2012.

9. Jürgen Habermas describes how rational reconstructions of the making process can contribute to self knowledge by raising an unconsciously functioning rule system to consciousness. 'It renders explicit the intuitive knowledge that is given with competence with respect to the rules in the form of "know how"' (1979: 23).

10. The comment 'not yet' points to the prospect of routinely encoding yet more rules into the

digital design and manufacturing media, so that the context is enough for an expert system to decide the size, position and material.

chapter 2: bending rules

1. Hermeneutics (Gadamer 1976) is the art, skill, theory, and philosophy of interpretation and understanding, especially in relation to reading texts but also in interpreting and making designs, and indeed all products, processes and phenomena. Philosophical hermeneutics is particularly associated with the German philosopher Hans-Georg Gadamer (1900–2002). See Snodgrass and Coyne 2006: 35–40.

2. Andrew Harrison notes that it is a philosophical commonplace that in the case of verbal expression, one certainly does not need to run through the silent conclusion that one ought to say something or other—one 'straightway speaks' (1978: 44).

3. Compare philosopher Richard Rorty writing about vocabulary in the way that concepts are described, emphasizing the link between language and thought: 'Interesting philosophy is rarely an examination of the pros and cons of a thesis. Usually it is, implicitly or explicitly, a contest between an entrenched vocabulary, which has become a nuisance and a half-formed new vocabulary which vaguely promises great things' (1989: 9).

4. Using Flash and proprietary code, Joshua Davis (by default) pioneered a rule-based approach to interactive abstract expression for Web design as displayed in the extensive archives on his site. His digital design approach begins with the seed of an idea that develops contingently in conjunction with computer code as described in his book *Flash to the Core* (Davis 2003).

5. To show that law is only understood in its application, Gadamer cites Aristotle's concept of equity (*epiekeikeia*), the correction or accommodation of the law. Aristotle says that no law has a straightforward and clear-cut meaning but has a certain internal tension in that it can be applied in a number of ways (Snodgrass 1991: 2). Mitchell supports this view of rules in design when he writes 'designers both apply and construct them, in much the same way that courts both apply and construct the law by engaging specific contexts of application' (1990: 238).

6. See for example Generator.x at http://www. generatorx.no for art and design works that conform to codified computer rules sets and systems. Generator.x was created in 2005 as the result of a series of conversations between Marius Watz and Atle Barcley. The manifesto of this group states,

> Computational strategies are having an impact in many creative fields. Generator.x was set up to examine the following topics in particular: Generative aesthetics: How can generative strategies successfully be applied to aesthetic problems? Whether the aim is provide a design solution or simply to explore the dynamic qualities of a given system, the process requires translating intuitive creative choices into rules and machine-readable code. What are the criteria for an interesting solution, what parameters and boundary conditions can be manipulated to produce satisfying results? Designing processes: A computational approach to design changes static objects into dynamic processes. What implications does this have for design and architecture, whether used for analysis, aesthetic expression or information visualization? Performative software: Musicians and visual performers are using generative systems to create custom software instruments for live performance, as well as to produce direct synaesthetic mappings between sound and image. How can a software instrument approach the complexity and expressive range of a physical instrument

that has been perfected over centuries? Software by creatives for creatives: Artists and designers are increasingly creating their own software to meet special needs not covered by commercial packages, sharing their results as Open Source. ('Products of Play' 2008)

7. Michael Ostwald (2010) discusses the ethical issues that arise in the uses of auto-generative design processes in architecture.

8. For example, Gehry Technologies' Digital Project system for buildings offers a 'knowledge template' to 'capture' patterns and sequences of operations for adaptation and re-use. 'A flexible repeated design element can automatically adjust its shape and dimensions when it is placed at multiple locations within a complex building system' (Gehry Technologies 2010) or is re-used on multiple projects.

chapter 3: making digital artefacts

1. In 2012 some typical examples are AutoCad for 2D drafting; FormZ, Rhino and 3D Studio Max for 3D modelling; ArchiCad, Bentley and Revit specifically for building modelling.

2. See the Web site for Sagmeister Inc, http:// www.sagmeister.com, accessed 28 Apr. 2012.

3. For an interview with Massimo Vignelli of Vignelli Associates, see http://www.designboom. com/eng/interview/vignelli.html, accessed 28 Apr. 2012.

4. In another field, the art market seems to expect a consistent style of work, a distinctive personal grammar: 'On the one hand, there is this notion of pluralism, which ordinarily calls up the idea of freedom, a climate of unfettered creative expression, and so forth. On the other hand, however, there is the idea that precisely because of this pluralism, there was a need to establish a "monotheistic thing" in one's work so as to be able to construct a unified artistic identity and to differentiate oneself from those seeking to do the same' (Freeman 1993: 192). Freeman quotes Hauser (1979: 508) as suggesting that 'the specialisation of painters in particular genres is one of the most important results of the trade in works of art to develop since the end of the Renaissance' arising because 'art dealers are constantly demanding the same sort of work by their suppliers, ones which have shown themselves to be most economically viable.' The same could be said for the contemporary international star architect market, with architects being chosen for so-called iconic buildings expected to deliver a product in their established style.

chapter 4: developing digital creativity

1. To be encouraged and recognized, creativity must be valued. In societies where knowledge and cultural lore are transmitted orally, creative ideas spread slowly and a creative interpretation of tradition threatens society. Creativity was spurred by the invention of the printing press, and is spurred again by the speed and accessibility of the Internet (Csikszentmihalyi 1999).

2. Gardner (1993: 29) contrasts ' "little c" creativity—the sort which all of us evince in our daily lives—and "big C" creativity—the kind of breakthrough which occurs only very occasionally' (qtd in Nickerson 1999: 399).

3. Briskman (1981) credits Stanley Eveling as influential in the way he sees creativity.

4. Koestler's emphasis on association of ideas or frames is paralleled by other writers—see Brown (1989).

5. Antony Palmer discusses the view that if the creativity of a process can be explained, it cannot be creative.

Understanding the creativity of a piece of work presents the dilemma that if the account we give is successful it will have the effect of denying that creativity is involved . . . If the same is pointed to in denying creativity as in giving an account of it, it is not surprising that it tends to disappear with its own account. The element of originality might still be left, of being the first to work in terms of certain principles, but then, to understand the creativity involved would be to understand how those principles came to be used and the dilemma returns. (1971, qtd in Harrison 1978: 68)

6. Sternberg writes that the investment theory of creativity 'is a confluence theory according to which creative people are those who are willing and able to "buy low and sell high" in the realm of ideas . . . Buying low means pursuing ideas that are unknown or out of favour but that have growth potential. Often, when these ideas are first presented, they encounter resistance. The creative individual persists in the face of this resistance and eventually sells high, moving on to the next new or unpopular idea' (2006: 97–8; see also Sternberg and Lubart 1992).

7. A more extensive list is given in advice to British teachers of what to look for to recognize creativity in school children (Qualifications and Curriculum Authority 2009). The list applies equally to adults, including looking at ourselves.

8. The criteria for notable works were empirically defined: for composers, works for which five or more recordings were available at the time of the study; for artists, works reproduced in any one of eleven general histories of art; for poets, works included in the *Norton Anthology of Poetry* at the time of the study.

9. Past work is framed by a designer's worldview, which is dependent on the intelligence invoked in any contingent event. For Howard Gardner (1999), there are at least eight forms of intelligence, so any person's creative potential may be understood as greater than that revealed by a conventional IQ test.

10. Tim Harford (2010) cites two examples from aviation: the highly successful British World War II Spitfire fighter developed by the small company Supermarine, and the radical US U-2 spy plane and Stealth fighters developed by a deliberately separated skunk works at Lockheed.

11. Csikszentmihalyi notes that many people opt out of this kind of almost obsessive creativity-focused lifestyle, while others persevere. 'In our longitudinal study of artists . . . some of the potentially most creative persons stopped doing art and pursued ordinary occupations, while others who seemed to lack creative potential persevered and eventually produced works of art that were hailed as important creative achievements' (1999: 313).

12. Csikszentmihalyi makes a similar point about authority in science: 'the opinion of a very small number of leading university professors was enough to certify that Einstein's ideas were creative' (1999: 315).

chapter 5: analysis

1. Dean Bruton recalls that his first reading of the grammar of one of artist-designer-mathematician Lionel March's paintings was based on a reading of positive shapes on a green background. From March's perspective, this reading was flawed because it misunderstood the basis of the work. Once March explained that his approach used classes of grids (1981) and that his imagery was based on the orientation of stripes conceived with 'point-set theory as its generative grammar', new understanding of his painting emerged with alternative readings. March wrote, 'My works were rule-bound in a way not determined by logic alone' (1981: 242).

2. Arne Jacobsen's architectural works include the SAS Royal Hotel in Copenhagen (1959) and St Catherine's College in Oxford (1963). His chairs (for Fritz Hansen A/S), cutlery (also for Stelton A/S), VOLA taps (for I. P. Lund), and lamps (for Louis Poulson A/S) are as famous as the Cylinda-Line tableware.

3. In 1980 Robert T. Buck Jr, director of the Albright-Knox Art Gallery, described them as 'among the major contributions of the past decade to contemporary American painting' (1980: 42).

4. Information about *white.sands* and other examples of Alvy Ray Smith's art can be seen on his Web pages at http://alvyray.com/Art/default.htm, accessed 11 Jan. 2011.

5. Benoît Mandelbrot (1924–) is considered to be the key figure in the field of fractal geometry. His best-known book is *The Fractal Geometry of Nature* (1982).

chapter 7: serious play

1. Those engaged in the studios were undergraduate or postgraduate coursework students. The notion of setting game-like tasks for design students is common, although the explicit linking with grammar is less common. Terry Knight's work in architecture and design at UCLA and MIT established a framework for the exploration of shape grammars in studio practice (Knight 1994). Her work with students developed innovative design using formal applications of rule systems. The success of her work inspired others to experiment in their own studio practice. Much was done in schools of architecture. For example, Jerzy Wojtowicz and William Fawcett at the University of Hong Kong in the 1980s adopted a formal approach using concepts of shape grammars (Wojtowicz and Fawcett 1986), and Robert and Rivka Oxman with Antony Radford at the University of Sydney explored the analysis and generation of architectural plans (Oxman, Radford and Oxman 1989).

2. Of course, a grammatical studio is not limited to the virtual digital realm. We have played with physical models as well. By exploring language and form relationships with materials such as wood, metals, glass and plastic, we could construct maquettes and sculptural installations using a grammatical approach. The games described in this chapter could also be extended by making 3D prints from the digital models.

chapter 8: studio journals

1. This example is typical of a transition period where the design and construction workflow is not integrated and combines old and new media. As noted already in this book, there are compelling reasons to shift to building information modelling even at this small scale. Repetitive housing units are particularly suited to techniques of building information modelling and mass customization.

2. For the Thiel House 1997–9, see 'The Sanctuary', http://www.architecturemedia.com/aa/ aaissue.php?issueid=199903&article=8&typ eon=2, accessed 28 Apr. 2012. For the Hammond House 1993–4, see 'Hammond House, Cooran' in *Australian Achievement in Architecture Awards*, http://www.architecturemedia.com/aa/aaissue. php?issueid=201003&article=13&typeon=2, accessed 28 Apr. 2012.

3. Making materials visible is often expensive, because of the construction care needed to make visible joints and connections presentable rather than hidden away behind linings and cover plates. The selective in this rule signifies that materials would only be expressed in places, as if the lining material had occasionally been left off to reveal the construction behind.

chapter 9: critical ideas

1. In this book we have concentrated on the processes and media of design, and not on the ethical, environmental and social reasons and contexts for design. It is these contexts that should drive and motivate design, not the media—but that would be another book.

annotated guide to further reading

There are many books relevant to digital design. Here we list a few of our favourites that develop or complement the themes of our book. We do not include any of the genre of how-to books that lead their readers through the processes of learning to use and exploit specific software—though important, they tend to have a short shelf life because software continually changes.

Burry, J., and Burry, M. (2010), *The New Mathematics of Architecture*, New York: Thames & Hudson.
  The word 'Architecture' in the title labels the field in which 'the new mathematics' is explored, but the themes apply in many form-making design fields. Jane and Mark Burry are architects who have engaged in the practical application of these concepts, most notably in Mark's work on the completion of the Church of the Sagrada Familia in Barcelona, designed by the Catalan architect Antoni Gaudí, with construction beginning in 1882. In this book they classify the mathematics involved into six themes: mathematical surfaces and seriality; chaos, complexity, emergence; packing and tiling; optimization; topology; datascapes and multidimensionality. Mostly, it is the ability to exploit the mathematics with computers that is new, not the mathematical concepts themselves. Each theme is lucidly introduced and then illustrated by case studies from contemporary architecture. There is also an excellent glossary, where terminology is explained with diagrams as well as text.

Calleja, G. (2011), *In-Game: From Immersion to Incorporation*, Cambridge: MIT Press.
  Rather than seeing immersion in a digital game as a singular experience, Gordon Calleja advocates and explains 'incorporation' as a more specific phenomenon involving six dimensions of player involvement: kinesthetic, spatial, shared, narrative, affective and ludic (playfulness).

Cross, N. (2006), *Designerly Ways of Knowing* (Board of International Research in Design), London: Springer Verlag.
  Cross outlines the key historical developments in the theory of design and offers insights into the designer's dialogue between process and product.

Elam, K. (2001), *Geometry of Design: Studies in Proportion and Composition*, New York: Princeton Architectural Press.
  Kimberley Elam provides a foundation for designers interested in proportioning systems for products, and demonstrates how the science of measurement might be used.

Fryer, C., Noel, S., and Rucki, E. (eds) (2008), *Digital by Design: Crafting Technology for Products and Environments*, London: Thames and Hudson.
  This is a well-illustrated compendium of over 100 examples of products, art installations and environments created through digital design, with contributions by many designers. Unlike our book, it does not present a coherent theoretical position, but like our book, it links design with art.

Hemmerling, M., and Tiggemann, A. (2011), *Digital Design Manual*, Berlin: DOM.
  Marco Hemmerling and Anke Tiggemann introduce digital tools with examples and tutorials based on everyday practice. The field is architecture and urban design, but much of the book is

relevant to other design fields and especially relevant to making environments for film and games. It is more practical than our book, without the emphasis on a way of thinking.

Holzman, S. (1994), *Digital Mantras*, Cambridge, MA: MIT Press.

Quite old now, but Steve Holzman's enjoyable book draws attention (with a mystical bent) to structure and rules in nature, art, music and other forms of creative work, and develops a personal philosophy of creativity and expression in the digital age that draws on examples from the past.

Iwamoto, L. (2009), *Digital Fabrications: Architectural and Material Techniques*, New York: Princeton Architectural Press.

Lisa Iwamoto is an accomplished designer who organizes this highly illustrated book around form-making techniques of sectioning, tessellating, folding, contouring and forming. The book explains the thinking behind the work of a group of emerging (meaning not the currently most famous names, and usually much younger than the famous) international designer-architects. Like those discussed in *The New Mathematics of Architecture*, the techniques are relevant to designers outside architecture, and many of the examples come from interior design and temporary installations.

Lupton, E. (2010), *Thinking with Type: A Critical Guide for Designers, Writers, Editors, & Students*, 2nd revised and expanded edition, New York: Princeton Architectural Press.

Ellen Lupton provides a foundational guide for the understanding of digital typography by outlining the rules and principles of design in graphics.

Schön, D. (1982), *The Reflective Practitioner: How Professionals Think in Action*, New York: Basic Books.

Although thirty years old, Donald Schön's book still offers a remarkable explanation of the hermeneutic practice of professions in various fields, including architecture and planning. It is particularly useful in providing lots of examples of the use and adaption of patterns taken from the professional's storehouse of previous experiences and acquired expertise. Schön wrote before digital media impacted the fields he describes, but his analysis is no less relevant.

Woodbury, R. F. (2010), *Elements of Parametric Design*, Oxford and New York: Routledge.

Robert Woodbury leads readers through the ideas, reasons, techniques and mathematics for parametric design, written by an enthusiast who gives lucid explanations. Like this book, *Digital Design: A Critical Introduction*, Woodbury's book embraces the idea of design patterns and recognizes that exploiting the potential involves a way of thinking that is symbiotic with the tools. As well as mathematical descriptions and algorithms, there are some convincing case studies of parametric design in architecture.

references

Adams, J. (1990), *Conceptual Blockbusting: A Guide to Better Ideas*, 2nd ed., London: Basic Books.

Alexander, C., Ishikawa, S., Silverstein, M., with Jacobson, M., Fiksdahl-King, I., and Angel, S. (1977), *A Pattern Language*, Oxford: Oxford University Press.

Amabile, T.M. (1983), *The Social Psychology of Creativity*, New York: Springer.

Arnheim, R. (1969), *Visual Thinking*, Berkley: University of California Press.

As, I., and Schodek, D. (2008), *Dynamic Digital Representations in Architecture: Visions in Motion*, London: Taylor and Francis.

Bentley, P. (1999), *Evolutionary Design by Computers*, San Francisco: Morgan Kaufman.

Berne, E. (1964), *Games People Play*, Harmondsworth: Penguin.

Bierut, M. (2011), 'Battle Hymn of the Tiger Mentor, or, Why Modernist Designers Are Superior', *Design Observer Group* (31 Jan. 2011), http://observatory.designobserver.com/entry.html?entry=24558, accessed 1 June 2011.

Boag, N. (1999), Personal communication to Antony Radford, Adelaide.

Bolliger, K., Grohmann, M., and Tessmann, O. (2010), 'Structured Becoming: Evolutionary Processes in Design Engineering', in R. Oxman and R. Oxman (eds), 'The New Structuralism', *Architectural Design*, 4: 34–9.

Briskman, L. (1981), 'Creative Product and Creative Process in Science and Art', in D. Dutton and M. Krausz (eds), *The Concept of Creativity in Science and Art*, The Hague: Martinus Nijhoff.

Brown, R.T. (1989), 'Creativity: What Are We to Measure?', in J.A. Glover, R.R. Ronning and C.R. Reynolds (eds), *Handbook of Creativity*, New York: Plenum Press.

Bruton, D. (1996), 'A Contingent Sense of Grammar', PhD thesis, University of Adelaide.

Bruton, D. (2007), 'Fusing Horizons: A Grammatical Design Approach for the Arts and Humanities: Using Rules, Contingency and Hermeneutics in Design Education', *Arts and Humanities in Higher Education*, 6/3: 309–27.

Bruton, D. (2010), 'International Perspectives on Animation in Higher Education', ConnectED2010—2nd International Conference on Design Education, 28 June–1 July, Sydney, 127–35, http://connected2010.eproceedings.com.au/abstracts.html, accessed 9 Jan. 2011.

Bruton, D. (2011), 'Learning Creativity and Design for Innovation', *International Journal of Technology and Design Education,* 21/3: 321–33.

Buck, R.T. (1980), *Richard Diebenkorn*, Buffalo, NY: Rizzoli.

Burry, M. (2006), 'Parametric Design, Associative Geometry', in A. Chaszar (ed.), *Blurring the Lines*, Chichester: Wiley-Academy.

Burry, M., and Burry, J. (2010), *The New Mathematics of Architecture*, London: Thames & Hudson.

Calleja, G. (2011), *In-Game: From Immersion to Incorporation*, Cambridge, MA: MIT Press.

Chaszar, A. (ed.) (2006), *Blurring the Lines*, Chichester: Wiley-Academy.

Chermayeff, S., and Alexander, C. (1963), *Community and Privacy*, New York: Doubleday (republished, Harmondsworth: Pelican Books, 1966).

Cohen, H. (2010), 'Driving the Creative Machine (Creativity, Cognition and Computers in the Visual

Arts)', Crossroads Lecture, 26 Sept., Eastsound, WA: Orcas Center (unpublished).

Cook, D.A. (1996), *A History of Narrative Film*, New York: W.W. Norton.

Corning, P.A. (2002), 'The Re-Emergence of "Emergence": A Venerable Concept in Search of a Theory', *Complexity*, 7/6: 18–30, http://dx.doi.org/10.1002/cplx.10043, accessed 28 Apr. 2012.

Coyne, R. (1996), Interview, 2 Aug. in Edinburgh by Dean Bruton, PhD thesis, University of Adelaide.

Craig, B. (2012). 'FAQ', *Filmmaking.net*, http://www.filmmaking.net/faq/answers/faq189.asp?catid=4, accessed 30 Apr. 2012.

Crawford, C. (2005), *On Interactive Storytelling*, Berkeley, CA: New Riders Games.

Cross, N. (2006), *Designerly Ways of Knowing* (Board of International Research in Design), London: Springer Verlag.

Csikszentmihalyi, M. (1988), 'Society, Culture, and Person: A Systems View of Creativity', in R.J. Sternberg (ed.), *The Nature of Creativity*, New York: Cambridge University Press.

Danto, A. (1997), *Encounters and Reflections: Art in the Historical Present*, Berkeley: University of California Press.

Davis, G.A. (1983), *Creativity Is Forever*, Dubuque, IA: Kendall/Hunt.

Davis, J. (2003), *Flash to the Core: Interactive Sketchbook*, Indianapolis: New Riders.

De Bono, E. (2007), *How to Have a Beautiful Mind*, London: Ebury Press.

Deicher, S. (2010), *Piet Mondrian: 1872–1944; Structures in Space (Basic Art)*, New York: Taschen.

Diaz, J. (2008), '1960s Braun Products Hold the Secrets to Apple's Future', *Gizmodo.com*, http://gizmodo.com/343641/1960s-braun-products-hold-the-secrets-to-apples-future, accessed 28 Apr. 2012.

Duchamp, M. (1957), 'The Creative Act', lecture to the convention of the American Federation of the Arts, Houston, April, in R. Lebel (1959), *Marcel Duchamp*, New York: Paragraphic Books.

Dutton, D., and Krausz, M. (eds) (1981), *The Concept of Creativity in Science and Art*, The Hague: Martinus Nijhoff.

Elam, K. (2001), *Geometry of Design: Studies in Proportion and Composition*, New York: Princeton Architectural Press.

Eliot, T.S. (1920), *The Sacred Wood: Essays on Poetry and Criticism*, London: Methuen.

Emmerling, L. (2003), *Jackson Pollock*, Köln: Taschen.

Fish, S. (1985), 'Consequences', in W.J.T. Mitchell (ed.), *Against Theory: Literary Studies and the New Pragmatism*, Chicago: University of Chicago Press.

Flemming, U. (1996), 'Review Essay: Good, Not So Good, and Everything in Between: Current Work on Computational Creativity', *Environment and Planning B: Planning and Design*, 23/2: 242–3.

Fox, W. (2006), *A Theory of General Ethics: Human Relationships, Nature, and the Built Environment*, MIT Press: Cambridge, MA.

Freeman, M. (1993), *Finding the Muse. A Sociopsychological Inquiry into the Conditions of Artistic Creativity*, Cambridge: Cambridge University Press.

Froebel, F. (1912), *Froebel's Chief Writings on Education*, trans. S.S.F. Fletcher and J. Welton, London: Arnold, http://core.roehampton.ac.uk/digital/froarc/frochi/, accessed 28 Apr. 2012.

Fryer, C., Noel, S., and Rucki, E. (eds) (2008), *Digital by Design: Crafting Technology for Products and Environments*, London: Thames & Hudson.

Gadamer, H.G. (1976), *Philosophical Hermeneutics*, trans. D. Ling, Los Angeles: University of California Press.

Gardner, H. (1993), *Creating Minds*, New York: Basic Books.

Gardner, H. (1999), *Intelligence Reframed*, New York: Basic Books.

Gehry, F.O. (2002), 'Frank Gehry Asks "Then What?"', interview by R.S. Wurman, http://www.ted.com/talks/frank_gehry_asks_then_what.html, accessed 28 Apr. 2012.

Gehry Partners (2010), Homepage, http://www.foga. com, accessed 28 Apr. 2012.

Gehry Technologies (2010), Homepage, http://www. gehrytechnologies.com, accessed 28 Apr. 2012.

Gips, J., and Stiny, G. (1980), 'Production Systems and Grammars: A Uniform Characterisation', *Environment and Planning B: Planning and Design*, 7: 399–408.

Glaser, M. (2011), *DesignBoom,* http://www.design boom.com/eng/interview/glaser.html, accessed 17 Feb. 2011.

Glover, J. A., Ronning, R. R., and Reynolds, C. R. (1989), *Handbook of Creativity*, New York: Plenum Press.

Grant, B. K. (2007), *Film Genre: From Iconography to Ideology*, London: Wallflower Press.

Griffiths, G. (2010), 'Eternal Optimism? Ethics Explained Away', Paper presented to Nordic Association of Architectural Research conference, Tampere, 22–24 Apr.

Grimshaw, N. (1998), Verbal response to a question at the Royal Australian Institute of Architects National Conference, Cairns, Australia, Oct.

Habermas, J. (1979), *Communication and the Evolution of Society*, Boston: Beacon Press.

Hanson, N.R.L., and Radford, A. D. (1986), 'Living on the Edge: A Grammar for Some Country Houses by Glenn Murcutt', *Architecture Australia*, 7: 66–73.

Harford, T. (2010), 'How a So-Called "Skunk Works" Project, Isolated from the Mainstream, Can Turn into Something Revolutionary', *BA Business Life*, 7: 6, http://www.babusinesslife.com/Tools/ Economics/The-evolution-of-skunk-works-.html, accessed 5 Sept. 2010.

Harrison, A. (1978), *Making and Thinking*, Hassocks: Harvester Press.

Hauser, A. (1979), *The Sociology of Art*, Chicago: University of Chicago Press.

Hayes, J.R. (1989). 'Cognitive Processes in Creativity', in J. A. Glover, R. R. Ronning and C. R. Reynolds (eds), *Handbook of Creativity*, New York: Plenum Press.

Hemmerling, M., and Tiggemann, A. (2011), *Digital Design Manual*, Berlin: DOM.

Herrnstein Smith, B. (1988), *Contingencies of Value*, London: Harvard University Press.

Holtzman, S. (1994), *Digital Mantras*, Cambridge: MIT Press.

Holzer, D., and Downing, S. (2010), 'Optioneering: A New Basis for Engagement between Architects and Their Collaborators', in R. Oxman and R. Oxman (eds), 'The New Structuralism', *Architectural Design*, 80/4: 61–3.

Huizinga, J. (1970), *Homo-Ludens: A Study of the Play Element in Culture*, London: Paladin.

Hurson, T. (2008), *Think Better: An Innovator's Guide to Productive Thinking*, New York: McGraw-Hill.

Iwamoto, L. (2009), *Digital Fabrications: Architectural and Material Techniques*, New York: Princeton Architectural Press.

Jobs, S. (2005), Stanford Commencement Address, Stanford University, http://tech.fortune.cnn.com/ 2010/02/24/steve-jobs-is-55, accessed 26 July 2010.

Johnson, P. A. (1994), *The Theory of Architecture*, New York: Van Nostrand Reinhold.

Karatani, K. (1965), *Architecture as Metaphor: Language, Number, Money*, Cambridge: MIT Press.

Kirsch, J.L., and Kirsch, R.A. (1986), 'The Structure of Paintings: Formal Grammar and Design', *Environment and Planning B: Planning and Design*, 13: 163–76.

Kirsch, J. L., and Kirsch, R. A. (1988), 'The Anatomy of Painting Style: Description with Computer Rules', *Leonardo*, 21/4: 437–44.

Kirsch, R. A. (1964), 'Computer Interpretation of English Text and Picture Patterns', IEEE Trans, *Electronic Computers,* 13: 363–76.

Kirsch, R.A., and Kirsch, J.L. (1996), Interview 23 July in Clarksburg, MD, by Dean Bruton, PhD thesis, University of Adelaide.

Kneller, G. F. (1965), *The Art and Science of Creativity*, New York: Holt, Reinhart and Winston.

Knight, T. (1994), *Transformations in Design*, Cambridge: MIT Press.

Knight, T. (1996), Interview 13 July in Boston by Dean Bruton, PhD thesis, University of Adelaide.

Koestler, A. (1964), *The Act of Creation*, London: Hutchinson.

Koestler, A. (1981), *Janus: A Summing Up*, London: Pan.

Kress, G., and van Leeuwen, T. (1996), *Reading Images: The Grammar of Visual Design*, London: Routledge.

Lansdown, J., and Earnshaw, R.A. (1989), *Computers in Art, Design and Animation*, New York: Springer-Verlag.

Lawson, B.R. (1980), *How Designers Think*, London: Architectural Press.

Lawson, B.R. (2004), *What Designers Know*, Oxford: Architectural Press.

Lindsay, B. (2001), *Digital Gehry*, Basel: Birkhäuser.

Linhart, S. (1998), *Mondrimat*, http://www.stephen.com/mondrimat, accessed 24 Dec. 2010.

Lloyd, D. (2004), 'A Brief History of the iPod', *iLounge*, 26 June, http://www.ilounge.com/index.php/articles/comments/instant-expert-a-brief-history-of-ipod, accessed 20 July 2010.

LucasArts (2007), 'The New Technology of the Force Unleashed: What Is Euphoria?', http://www.lucasarts.com/games/theforceunleashed/gameinfo/news/technology.html, accessed 27 Aug. 2007.

Lucie-Smith, E. (1984), *The Thames & Hudson Dictionary of Art Terms*, London: Thames & Hudson.

Lupton, E. (2010), *Thinking with Type: A Critical Guide for Designers, Writers, Editors, and Students*, 2nd revised and expanded ed., New York: Princeton Architectural Press.

Lye, J. (1996), 'Some Principles of Phenomenological Hermeneutics', http://www.brocku.ca/english/courses/4F70/ph.php, accessed 8 Jan. 2011.

Maeda, J. (2011), *designboom*, http://www.designboom.com/eng/interview/maeda.html, accessed 17 Feb. 2011.

Mandelbrot, B.B. (1982), *The Fractal Geometry of Nature*, New York: W.H. Freeman.

Manjoo, F. (2010), 'Inside the Secret World of Steve Jobs', *Times Magazine*, 24 July: 26–32.

Manovich, L. (2001), *The Language of New Media*, Cambridge: MIT Press.

March, L. (ed.) (1976), *The Architecture of Form: Cambridge Urban and Architectural Studies*, Cambridge: Cambridge University Press.

March, L. (1981), 'A Class of Grids', *Environment and Planning B,* 8: 325–32.

March, L. (1996), Interview, 3 July in Los Angeles by Dean Bruton, PhD thesis, University of Adelaide.

March, L., and Stiny, G. (1985), 'Spatial Systems in Architecture and Design: Some History and Logic', *Environment and Planning B*, 12/1: 31–53.

McCullough, M. (1998), *Abstracting Craft: The Practiced Digital Hand*, Cambridge: MIT Press.

Michalko, M. (2001), *Cracking Creativity,* Berkeley, CA: Ten Speed Press.

Miller, C.H. (2004), *Digital Storytelling: A Creator's Guide to Interactive Entertainment*, Oxford: Elsevier.

Miranda, E.R., and Wanderley, M.M. (2006), *New Digital Musical Instruments: Control and Interaction beyond the Keyboard*, Middleton: A-R Editions.

Mitchell, W. (1990), *The Logic of Architecture,* London: MIT Press.

Mitchell, W.J. (1995), *City of Bits*, Cambridge: MIT Press.

Nickerson, R. (1999), 'Enhancing Creativity', in R.J. Sternberg (ed.), *Handbook of Creativity*, Cambridge: Cambridge University Press.

Norman, D.A. (1988), *The Psychology of Everyday Things*, Cambridge: MIT Press.

Ostwald, M. (2010), 'Ethics and the Auto-Generative Design Process', *Building Research and Information*, 38/4: 390–400.

Oxford English Dictionary (2011), On-line version, 2nd ed. 1989, http://www.oed.com, accessed 1 June 2011.

Oxman, R. (ed.) (2006a), Special Issue on Digital Design, *Design Studies,* 27/3.

Oxman, R. (2006b), 'Theory and Design in the First Digital Age', *Design Studies*, 27/3: 229–65.

Oxman, R., and Oxman, R. (eds) (2010), Special Issue on 'The New Structuralism', *Architectural Design*, 80/4.

Oxman, R., Radford, A., and Oxman, R. (1989), *The Language of Architectural Plans*, Canberra: RAIA Education Division.

Palmer, A. (1971), 'Creativity and Understanding', *Proceedings of the Aristotelian Society*, Sup. vol., July.

Parnes, S.J. (1967), *Creative Behaviour Guidebook*, New York: Charles Scribner & Sons.

Pour-Hashemi, R. (2002), '*Citizen Kane* (1941)', *The Digital Fix*, http://film.thedigitalfix.com/content/id/4180/citizen-kane.html, accessed 20 Apr. 2011.

Prenksy, M. (2001), 'Digital Natives, Digital Immigrants', *On the Horizon,* 5 Oct., http://www.marcprensky.com/writing/Prensky%20-%20Digital%20Natives,%20Digital%20Immigrants%20-%20Part1.pdf, accessed Apr. 2012.

'Products of Play' (2008), 'Art from Code—Generator.x', *Generator.x*, http://www.generatorx.no/generatorx-introduction, accessed 1 Jan. 2011.

Prusinkiewicz, P., and Lindenmayer, A. (1990), *The Algorithmic Beauty of Plants*, Berlin: Springer-Verlag, http://algorithmicbotany.org/papers/#abop, accessed 13 June 2011.

Qualifications and Curriculum Authority (2009), 'How Can You Spot Creativity?', http://curriculum.qca.org.uk, accessed 20 Feb. 2009.

Radford, A.D. (2000), 'Games and Learning about Form in Architecture', *Automation in Construction*, 9/4: 379–85.

Rorty, R. (1989), *Contingency, Irony and Solidarity*, New York: Cambridge University Press.

Sagmeister, S. (2006), *designboom,* http://www.designboom.com/eng/interview/sagmeister.html, accessed 17 Feb. 2011.

Salen, K., and Zimmerman, E. (2004), *Rules of Play*, Cambridge: MIT Press.

Sapir, E. (1921), *Language: An Introduction to the Study of Speech*, New York: Harcourt, Brace, www.bartleby.com/186, accessed 8 Jan. 2011.

Scheurer, F. (2010), 'Materialising Complexity', in R. Oxman and R. Oxman (eds), 'The New Structuralism', *Architectural Design*, 80/4: 86–93.

Schön, D. (1982), *The Reflective Practitioner: How Professionals Think in Action*, New York: Basic Books.

Schulze, S., and Gratz, I. (eds) (2011), *Apple Design*, Ostfildem: Hatje Cantz.

Scruton, R. (1979), *The Aesthetics of Architecture*, London: Methuen (republished, Princeton, NJ: Princeton University Press, 1980).

Simon, H. (1988), 'The Science of Design: Creating the Artificial', *Design Issues,* 4/1–2.

Simon, H.A., and Chase, W. (1973) 'Skill in Chess', *American Scientist*, 61: 394–403.

Smith, A.R. (1996), Internet interview, 3 Oct. by Dean Bruton, PhD thesis, University of Adelaide.

Smith, P.F. (1987), *Architecture and the Principle of Harmony*, London: RIBA Press.

Snodgrass, A. (1991), 'Hermeneutics and the Application of Design Rules', in *Gadamer Action and Reason: Conference on the Application of the Hermeneutic Philosophy of Hans-Georg Gadamer*, Sydney: University of Sydney.

Snodgrass, A., and Coyne, R. (2006), *Interpretation in Architecture: Design as a Way of Thinking*, Abingdon: Routledge.

Stelton (2002), *Celebrating Arne Jacobsen 100 Years*, Hellerup, Denmark: Stelton A/S.

Sternberg, R.J. (2006), 'The Nature of Creativity', *Creativity Research Journal*, 18/1: 87–98.

Sternberg, R.J., and Lubart, T.I. (1992), 'Buy Low and Sell High: An Investment Approach to Creativity', *Current Directions in Psychological Science*, 1: 1–5.

Sternberg, R.J., and Lubart, T.I. (1996), 'Investing in Creativity', *American Psychologist*, 51/7: 677–88.

Stewart, G. (2010), Interview broadcast on ABC1, Australia TV, 8 June.

Stiny, G. (2006), *Shape*, Cambridge: MIT Press.

Takemori, T. (2006), 'Conference Hall, DZ Bank Berlin', in A. Chaszar (ed.), *Blurring the Lines*, Chichester: Wiley-Academy.

3D World (2010), 'The Making of Avatar', *3D World*, 1: 30–3, http://www.3dworldmag.com/2010/11/16/the-making-of-avatar, accessed 1 Jan. 2011.

Torrance, E.P. (1977), *Creativity in the Classroom,* Washington DC: National Education Association.

Trowse, N. (2002), 'The Exclusionary Potential of Genre: Margery Kempe's Transgressive Search for a Deniable Pulpit', in R.M. Coe, L. Lingard and

T. Teslenko (eds), *The Rhetoric and Ideology of Genre*, Cresskill: Hampston Press.

Tzonis, T., and Lefaivre, L. (1986), *Classical Architecture: The Poetics of Order*, Cambridge: MIT Press.

Utzon, J. (1970), 'Additive Architecture', *Arkitektur*, 1: 1–48.

Utzon, J. (2009), *Jørn Utzon Logbook Nr. 5: Additive Architecture*, Copenhagen: Editions Blondal.

Valéry, P. (1922), 'The Graveyard by the Sea', http://en.wikisource.org/wiki/The_Graveyard_by_the_Sea, accessed 21 Jan. 2009.

Valéry, P. (1956), 'Man and Sea Shell', in *The Collected Works of Paul Valéry*, vol. 1, selected with an introduction by J.R. Lawler, Princeton, NJ: Princeton University Press.

Van Bruggen, C. (1997), *Frank O. Gehry Guggenheim Museum Bilbao*, New York: Solomon R. Guggenheim Foundation.

Venturi, R., and Scott-Brown, D. (1996), Interview, 20 July in Philadelphia by Dean Bruton, PhD thesis, University of Adelaide.

Vignelli, M. (n.d.), *The Vignelli Canon,* http://www.vignelli.com/canon.pdf, accessed Apr. 2012.

Walker, D. (1996), Interview, 1 July in London at the Open University by Dean Bruton, PhD thesis, University of Adelaide.

Weisberg, R. (1999), 'Creativity and Knowledge: A Challenge to Theories', in R.J. Sternberg (ed.), *Handbook of Creativity*, Cambridge: Cambridge University Press.

Wishbow, N. (1988), 'Creativity in Poets', unpublished doctoral dissertation, Carnegie-Mellon University, Pittsburgh.

Wojtowicz, J., and Fawcett, W. (1986), *Architecture: Formal Approach*, London: Academy Editions.

Woodbury, R.F. (1993), 'Grammatical Hermeneutics', *Architectural Science Review*, 36/2: 53–64.

Woodbury, R.F. (2010), *Elements of Parametric Design*, Oxford: Routledge.

Yellan, J. (1996), *Typo Survival Kit: For All Type Emergencies,* Fremantle: Press for Success.

glossary

Additive (in design)—form made by the addition of elements, usually members of a consistent vocabulary of parts.

Algorithm—a sequence of instructions for carrying out a procedure.

Associative geometry—geometry in which modification of one entity results in the automatic modification of dependent entities according to preestablished rules, a key requirement for parametric design.

BIM (building information modelling)—a 3D digital model of a building based on a database of objects that can be used to analyse and predict the building's behaviour and as a basis for costing, construction and building management.

Biomimetic design—design based on emulating principles and patterns found in nature.

Biomorphic—appearing similar to a biological (living) organism in form and appearance, usually as a result of biomimetic design.

Body space—space that can be occupied by the physical human body, in contrast to mind space (or virtual space) which is only occupied in the mind.

Boolean operations (on 2D shapes or 3D volumes)—a set of union (addition), intersecting and subtracting (nonintersecting) operations by which form can be modified.

CAD (computer aided design, or computer aided drafting)—the process of using software for design or for technical drafting.

CAM (computer aided manufacture)—the process of linking computers directly to machines in manufacturing products.

CNC (computer numeric controlled) machine—a machine tool that operates by digital instructions in contrast to hand (manual) controls. The digital instructions may be derived directly from data created during the design process and represented in a digital model.

Computational design—designing using computation (and hence usually computers), whether for aesthetic or analytical purposes; related to generative design.

Contingency (in design)—possible but unexpected situations that require modification to the design, or provision for such situations.

Customized products—products (including designs) that are made or altered to suit individual specifications or needs, as distinct from mass-produced products that are all the same.

Derivation (in design)—the formation of a design from another design or base. In computational and generative design, a derivation is produced by the application of rules or algorithms to a source design. This process can be repeated in a derivation sequence.

Design—as a verb, to design is to plan for the making of a (physical or virtual) object, either before the actual making or during the process of making. As a noun, a design is the outcome from such a process.

Digital—the generating, processing and storing of information in terms of two states (usually represented as 0 and 1). The term is used to embrace the electronic technology that operates digitally, and the design and other processes that exploit that technology.

Digital workflow—the process of work being developed and transferred from one module to another during a design and manufacture continuum.

Evolution—an evolutionary algorithm emulates the processes of Darwinian evolution to generate designs in an iterative computational process. It therefore has components of reproduction, mutation, recombination and selection. It is a form of generative design and of computational design. The term *evolution* is also used as a general metaphor for the way a design develops.

Expert system—software that uses representations of the kinds of knowledge that humans use in order to solve problems. A common kind of knowledge representation is similar to a production system in design with two parts: a precondition (or IF statement) and a consequence (or THEN statement).

Fractals—a term coined by Benoît Mandelbrot (see Mandelbrot 1982) to denote a character in natural phenomena such as coastlines, plants and clouds where the same patterns appear (at least approximately) when looked at in overview or detail (self-similarity).

Free form—a form developed without either physical constraints or simple mathematical geometries.

Generative design—the generation of designs by a set of rules or an algorithm, usually using computers. A generative design system usually contains both a means for creating design variations and a means for selecting between them.

GIS (geographic information system (or geospatial information system))—software that stores and manages information related to geographical location. The information can take many forms, including land uses, ownership and values, natural resources, population, history and possible futures. It may also include photographs and models of landform and buildings, so that a GIS system can, for example, embrace a model for visualizing urban form.

Grammar (in design)—the way in which a chosen vocabulary of parts is modified and combined in design compositions. A formal grammar as a generative design system has three parts: a vocabulary of elements; a set of transformation rules that transform structured arrangements of the elements into new structures; and an initial structure.

Grammatical design—a way of thinking about design that emphasizes grammar, or more formally in generative design, a paradigm based directly on a vocabulary of elements and transformational rules.

Hermeneutics (in design)—the art, skill, theory and philosophy of interpretation and understanding of design products, both completed products and during the design process.

Language (in design)—a term embracing grammar and meanings in design, akin to a style and the way products in that style are interpreted. Designing in the same grammar will result in designs that belong to the same language.

Mass customization—the use of flexible CAM processes to produce customized products, hence combining the low unit costs associated with mass production processes and the utility of an individual purpose-made product.

Mind space—an analogy between a human mind and physical space, where the mind can be occupied by ideas and imaginings in the same way as physical space can be occupied by objects. The term *frame of mind* refers to mental preconceptions, prejudices, attitudes and associated emotions that influence how humans interpret and respond to situations and things, including designs.

Module—an independent, self-contained unit that can be linked to other modules to construct a more complex system.

Open source (software)—often freely available, open source software is provided as computer code that can be studied and modified by users.

Optimization (in design)—the process of finding the best design when measured against a criterion or criteria. A design can usually be optimal for only one criterion (for example cost, mass or energy use). In design there are typically many criteria, so choice involves trade-offs.

Optioneering (in design)—the explicit exploration of options as a part of design and construction processes.

Parametric design—design that uses parametric models to create a family of possible designs from which the best or most appropriate can be selected. An individual design within the possibly infinite range of possibilities is called an *instance* of the design.

Parametric model—a digital model in which geometric and other attributes are related so that when one attribute changes others may also change as defined by these relationships. The variable attributes are called parameters and may be subject to constraints so that a dimension, for example, may have a maximum and minimum value. Using a parametric model, design modifications and the creation of a family of related designs can be completed very quickly as long as the desired outcomes fit within the scope of the model.

Pattern—a set of rules. The rules may not be spelled out in words, but they are implicit in the pattern. A recurring decorative design is one kind of pattern because it follows rules, but there are many other kinds of patterns.

Pixel graphics—images that are only represented as arrays of pixels (picture elements) with no representation of geometric attributes such as lines, polygons and solids.

Plug-in—a software component that enhances a larger software application in performing specific tasks.

Prefabrication—the practice of making components of a design away from the site of assembly of the whole design or earlier than the time of assembly of the whole design. It is most commonly used to prefabricate components of a building or structure in a factory where machinery and conditions are better than are available on the construction site.

Production system (in design)—a system that generates designs by executing productions. Productions have two parts: a precondition (or IF statement) and an action (or THEN statement). If a production's precondition can be matched in the current state of the design, then the production is said to be triggered. If a production's action is executed, it is said to have fired. A rule interpreter prioritizes the firing of productions when more than one is triggered. A production system in design is a form of generative design.

Rapid prototyping—the automatic construction of physical objects from a 3D digital model, usually using 3D printing technologies where the object is built up as a sequence of fused layers.

Rationalization (in design)—modifying freeform geometry to make the form more amenable to fabrication and construction. A well-known example is the rationalization of the free-form shells of Jørn Utzon's competition design for the Sydney Opera House to re-form them as segments of well-defined spheres which could then be constructed as assemblies of prefabricated ribs of constant curvature.

Rule (in design)—a rule that governs aspects of the design because of physics, regulations, conformity to a style, software capability or simply designers' choices. Rules in design need to be interpreted in the context of their use. Rules as designers' choices are often speculative and provisional, so they can be amended or abandoned.

Scripting—the use of sequences of instructions to control the way a software application operates, written by the software user in the application's scripting language to extend or control the outcomes. It is distinct from the core computer code of the software application. Scripting is important in parametric, computational and generative design processes.

Selective laser sintering—a form of rapid prototyping in which heat generated by a laser fuses powdered material layer by layer, each layer representing a cross section of the part. The movement of the laser is controlled using data from a digital model. When complete, loose powder is removed leaving the fused model. The results can be highly detailed and intricate.

Shape grammar—a production system that operates on shapes, with shape rules that define how an existing (part of a) shape can be transformed into a new (part of a) shape (see Gips and Stiny 1980; Stiny 2006).

Simulation (in design)—the imitation of the appearance or behaviour of a design in order to predict and evaluate the actual characteristics of the design. It usually refers to the use of a digital model in the simulation of a physical design proposal, but the model can be physical (as in simulating the performance of a yacht hull and keel with a scale model in a wave tank), or the design outcome can be digital (as in simulating the behaviour of a complex Web site using a simpler prototype).

Software—the application programs and operating systems used by a computer, as distinct from the physical electronic circuits and other components which constitute the computer hardware.

Subtractive (in design)—form made by the subtraction of elements or space, usually in computer software capable of performing Boolean operations on 2D surfaces or 3D solids.

Surreal—not as is normally expected, as in a dream.

Synecdoche—a figure of speech in which a part is used for the whole or the whole for a part.

Systems theory—the transdisciplinary study of systems in general, particularly relations between a system and its bigger contexts, and a system and its smaller subsystems.

Tectonics (in design)—the art and science of constructing form, particularly in architecture.

3D print—a three-dimensional object printed by laying down successive layers of material, usually to make (the whole or part of) a physical full-size product prototype or scale model from a digital model.

UIM (urban information model)—a larger-scale equivalent of a building information model, used for city planning. It represents the 3D geometry of urban form and may be linked to a geographic information system for the same area.

Vector graphics—images that are represented as lines (vectors) between endpoints, as distinct from pixel graphics.

Vocabulary (in design)—the set of elements or element choices (such as forms and materials) that characterize design outcomes.

index